Georges Salines chaired the victims' association 13onze15: Fraternité et Vérité and campaigned for the prevention of radicalisation. He is the author of *L'Indicible de A à Z* (Le Seuil, 2016).

Azdyne Amimour has worked in several trades, in commerce, sport and cinema. He is the father of Samy Amimour, one of the three terrorists from Bataclan.

WE STILL HAVE WORDS

A STORY OF HOPE AND FRIENDSHIP IN THE
SHADOW OF THE BATACLAN ATTACKS

GEORGES SALINES   AZDYNE
SALINES   AMIMOUR

SCRIBNER

LONDON NEW YORK SYDNEY TORONTO NEW DELHI

First published in France by Robert Laffont, 2020
First published in Great Britain by Scribner, an imprint of
Simon & Schuster UK Ltd, 2020
This paperback edition published by Scribner, an imprint of
Simon & Schuster UK Ltd, 2021

1 3 5 7 9 10 8 6 4 2

Simon & Schuster UK Ltd
1st Floor
222 Gray's Inn Road
London WC1X 8HB

www.simonandschuster.co.uk
www.simonandschuster.com.au
www.simonandschuster.co.in

Simon & Schuster Australia, Sydney
Simon & Schuster India, New Delhi

The author and publishers have made all reasonable efforts to contact copyright-
holders for permission, and apologise for any omissions or errors in the form of
credits given. Corrections may be made to future printings.

A CIP catalogue record for this book is available from the British Library

Paperback ISBN: 978-1-4711-9678-2
eBook ISBN: 978-1-4711-9677-5

Typeset in Bembo by M Rules
Printed in the UK by CPI Group (UK) Ltd, Croydon, CR0 4YY

Contents

Foreword by Jon Snow

The very idea that two fathers – one whose son had been involved in murdering the other man's daughter – could at some point find it within themselves to become friends sounds fanciful.

Last year I was in the rare position to be sent by my Channel 4 News editor to Paris not only to meet these two men but to interview them together. I was to learn how, amid their improbable friendship, underpinned by their mutual grief, they had managed to write this extraordinary book.

The terror attack on a rock concert in the Bataclan in Paris on 13 November 2015 killed 130 mainly young people. Georges Salines, sixty-two, had lost his beloved 28-year-old daughter Lola. She had been there to hear her favourite band – Eagles of Death Metal. Azdyne Amimour, seventy-two, had lost his son Samy, of the very same age. Samy had gone to the Bataclan to kill as many people as he could. As he did so, he was shot dead by armed police.

The security forces eventually killed all seven perpetrators. It was the worst violent loss of life in France since the Second World War.

I reported the aftermath of it from Paris at the time. Even the next morning, there was still a palpable sense of shock at the scene of the attack. Some people were laying flowers, others were on their knees in tears. The security forces and police were everywhere.

Four years on, I found myself on the Eurostar to Paris, preparing to meet both men as their book, *Il Nous Reste Les Mots,* was about to be published in France. At the hotel where I was to interview them, it was Georges who arrived first, Azdyne soon after. They had a quiet but evident ease with each other, despite the grief they showed as they spoke of their loss. They had contrasting backgrounds. Azdyne is Algerian. He became a shopkeeper and now owns a vegetarian restaurant. Georges is French, a doctor, and works in public health.

Azdyne was quieter than Georges and, perhaps understandably, did not want his face to be seen on camera. The account he gave was of Samy's happy childhood, then he went on to describe how his son became radicalised in his early twenties. Both men had reached out after their loss. They eventually met through the association for survivors of the Bataclan that Georges was instrumental in setting up.

Poignantly, the book ends with both of them writing to the other's dead child. Their book is an extraordinary insight into how the human spirit can bear so shattering a loss and find it within itself to forgive. Forgive, but not without castigating the grim ingredients that brought about so heinous an assault on other human beings.

Translator's Note

When I saw Georges Salines and Azdyne Amimour being interviewed on Channel 4 News on 14 January 2020, I was deeply moved by the courage and candour of these two fathers as they spoke about their book that had just been published in France. That a man whose daughter was killed in the attack on the Bataclan concert hall in Paris on 13 November 2015 should be ready to engage in thoughtful, reasoned and very public dialogue with the father of one of the terrorists who carried out the atrocity struck me, as it did many others, as both amazing and inspiring. It also convinced me that what they had to say needed to be made available to English-speaking readers.

The conversations that make up this book are not always comfortable reading: the topics and emotions they cover are harrowing and still raw. Yet, what comes across throughout is that these two men from such different backgrounds, one from southwest France, the other born in colonial-era

Algeria, have much more in common than just pain and regret. Both sons of the Mediterranean – for them not just a sea (*mer*) but almost a mother (*mère*) – they share a rich cultural heritage shaped by the French language, and visible in the way they use it. In translating their words, I have sought to communicate not only the nuances of the language they employ but also the unspoken references to this shared literary, musical, political and historical universe that simply go without saying for French speakers, but require some explanation for the rest of us.

What these two men also share is faith: Azdyne Amimour's faith, as a Muslim, in God's justice and forgiveness; Georges Salines' faith, as a man of science, in our human capacity for reason and truth. These converge in their very real and heartfelt commitment to the guiding Republican principles of *liberté, égalité, fraternité* – freedom, equality, fraternity – which have come to transcend France's various national divisions over the past two centuries.

It is the last and perhaps most complex of these – *fraternité* – that their words embody the most; indeed, it is part of the name of the organisation co-founded by Georges Salines to support victims of the attacks in Paris, *13onze15: Fraternité et Vérité* (13eleven15: Fraternity and Truth). 'Fraternity' in the sense of a non-negotiable brother- and sisterhood, a shared irreducible humanity that brings with it a responsibility towards one another, no matter what differences and tragedies divide us.

As I write this in Manchester, in the midst of a pandemic

which has laid bare our frailty and interdependence, it is three years to the day since our city suffered its own incomprehensible tragedy with the suicide attack that killed twenty-two people, including children, and injured hundreds more at the Manchester Arena. The need for fraternity, truth and justice is as urgent as ever, as is the central message of this book: may this never happen again.

Jonathan Hensher
Manchester
22 May 2020

For all those who have fallen
beneath bullets and bombs,
For all those who have survived
and have to continue their lives
with the effects of their injuries,
their traumatic memories,
the memory of the people they loved.
Let life be stronger than terror.

Georges Salines

For all the victims,
direct and indirect, of 13 November 2015.
For an end to resentment, may it be replaced by virtue.
For my family, who continue to be strong.

Azdyne Amimour

'Now that youth
Breathes its last breath upon the blue-tinged pane
Now that youth
Has betrayed me with mechanical disdain
Now that youth
You remember, don't you, remember . . .'

Louis Aragon, *Le Nouveau Crève-cœur*

('*Maintenant que la jeunesse / S'éteint au carreau
bleu / Maintenant que la jeunesse / Machinale m'a
trahi / Maintenant que la jeunesse / Tu t'en souviens
souviens-t'en . . .*')

'Tomorrow, at dawn,
at that hour when the land lies bleached,
I will set out. You see, I know you are waiting for me.
I will go through the forest, o'er high mountain reach.
Far from you, I can no longer bear to be. [. . .]
And when I arrive, I will place upon your tomb
A bouquet of green holly and heather in bloom.'

**Victor Hugo, '*Demain, dès l'aube . . .*',
*Les Contemplations***

('*Demain, dès l'aube, à l'heure où blanchit la campagne, / Je
partirai. Vois-tu, je sais que tu m'attends. / J'irai par la forêt,
j'irai par la montagne. / Je ne puis demeurer loin de toi plus
longtemps. [. . .] Et quand j'arriverai, je mettrai sur ta tombe /
Un bouquet de houx vert et de bruyère en fleur.*')

Foreword

Georges Salines lost his daughter Lola in the terror attack of 13 November 2015 at the Bataclan concert hall in Paris. An editor of children's and young adult books who was passionate about her work, Lola devoted her free time to her friends and to the things she loved: roller derby, travel, drawing and music. That evening, she had gone to listen to the concert by The Eagles of Death Metal. She was twenty-eight.

Born in Tarbes, in southwest France, she grew up in Martinique and Egypt, before moving with her family to Paris, the city she loved more than any other. Following her death, her father, Georges Salines, a public health physician in Paris, helped found the victims' support association 13eleven15: Fraternity and Truth (*13onze15: Fraternité et Vérité*) and was its first president. Today, he actively campaigns to prevent radicalisation and raise awareness of the mechanisms which can draw individuals towards extreme violence.

Azdyne Amimour is the father of Samy Amimour, one

of the three terrorists who carried out the Bataclan attack. Originally from Algeria, Azdyne has led many different lives, working in business, sport and the film industry. A free spirit whose life is spent on the move between France and Belgium, travelling is a way for him to seek to understand the terrible acts carried out by his son.

After starting a law degree at university, Samy Amimour gradually became radicalised, before disappearing overnight and resurfacing in Syria. He then made his way back into France unchallenged and took part in the hostage-taking at the Bataclan in which ninety people lost their lives, including Lola Salines. He was shot dead on the stage by a police officer. He was twenty-eight. Three days after the attack, his parents' home was raided, and Azdyne Amimour would learn from the state prosecutor himself that his son was one of the group of killers who carried out the attack on the concert venue.

How did Samy Amimour get back into France without being questioned? This is still a mystery. His father, who wanted to avoid such a tragedy ever happening, had already gone looking for his son in Syria. Today, he is trying to understand what happened by building links with survivors of the attack, and he still hopes one day to find his granddaughter, who is at present somewhere in Iraq or Syria. She is all that he has left of this son who was caught in the tentacles of the jihadist octopus.

How did we end up having to face such horror? On the night of 13 November 2015, the attacks on the Bataclan, the

Stade de France and restaurant terraces in eastern Paris left dozens of families in mourning and shook the entire world: 131 dead and several hundred wounded.

Following this night of terrorist violence, the worst in France's history, many grief-stricken loved ones and relatives have spoken of their terrible pain. To date, it has almost exclusively been women, mothers of jihadists, who have made their voices heard, giving their own testimony in order to try to prevent new atrocities, but few fathers have spoken. Certainly not two fathers who might have been expected to be poles apart: the father of a victim from the Bataclan and the father of one of the attackers.

Georges Salines and Azdyne Amimour met for the first time in February 2017 at Azdyne Amimour's request. In September 2018, the idea of producing a book based on their conversations was born.

Over the course of a series of interviews bringing the two men together, some extraordinarily painful topics were discussed. A family tragedy for the two fathers, the attacks of 13 November 2015 were also experienced as a national and international trauma. Some of the exchanges in this book thus inevitably contain a powerful emotional charge able to resonate with us all, regardless of who we are or where we are from. Sometimes the tone of the men's discussion is cordial, sometimes there are disagreements, but their conversation is based throughout on listening attentively to each other, in a spirit of deep mutual respect.

This book maps out the words which, together, with

courage and determination, Georges Salines and Azdyne Amimour have been able to exchange, and these must not be taken out of context. Through dialogue, they have sought to understand what happened, the better to prevent it from happening again, and to go beyond hatred.

Preface

Georges Salines (GS): I first met Azdyne Amimour before the idea of writing this book took form. He asked if we could meet in February 2017, when I was the president of 13eleven15: Fraternity and Truth (*13onze15: Fraternité et Vérité*), an organisation set up to support survivors and the families of victims of the Paris attacks of 13 November 2015. I must admit that, to begin with, I didn't quite know what to think. I asked him to be more specific about what we would be discussing, and he replied: 'I want to speak with you about this tragic event, as I feel that I am a victim too because of my son.' This brief answer stirred up contradictory thoughts in my mind.

I could understand how this man might feel that he was a victim. A few months earlier, in April 2016, I had attended a conference by the Quilliam Foundation, a British think tank founded by the former Islamist Maajid Nawaz that focuses on counter-extremism, and on tackling Islamism and jihadism. This event brought together a large number of European organisations around the theme of 'FATE' (Families Against Terrorism and Extremism). The part of the conference which had left a particularly deep impression on me was a session where the mothers of jihadists were invited to speak. I had been so moved that I included an entry on these women in my book, *The Unspeakable: An A to Z* (*L'Indicible de A à Z*):

These women have lost their children, even though they are still alive. They have seen them change into people that they no longer recognise. [...] They also carry a terrible burden of guilt. Yet many of their stories do not conform to the usual clichés. They were loving mothers who did their best to bring their children up well, mothers who were neither violent, abusive nor absent. Now they are striving to protect the brothers and sisters who are left behind, who don't understand the situation and, in the case of the youngest children, are sometimes frightened when the police come to search the family home. Many of them work with charities and other organisations in the fight against terrorism.[1]

So, hearing the word 'victim' applied to the parents of jihadists did not shock me. In *The Unspeakable*, I had even used it to describe my daughter's murderers, explaining why I felt no hatred towards these victims of their own madness and of their recruiters, but victims who had consented to

---

1 Georges Salines, *L'Indicible de A à Z*, Seuil, 2016.

carry out a terrible crime, and who are therefore guilty. The fact remains that they are victims who have lost their own lives by taking the lives of others, without gaining anything in return – least of all a place in paradise.

Looking at the question rationally, however, I was able to see that the parents of jihadists could not be presumed guilty by default. Some, as seems to have been the case for certain members of the family of Mohammed Merah – the jihadist who killed seven people, including three Jewish children, in southwestern France in 2012 – were complicit, ideologically speaking at least. Others were not, and the latter seem to form the vast majority. Nevertheless, meeting the father of the man who may well have personally murdered my daughter was a far more uncomfortable prospect than speaking with the mothers of young men who had gone to Syria, and whose actions had not affected me directly.

My own feelings aside, there were other difficult questions. Given that Monsieur Amimour saw himself as a victim, would he ask to join our organisation, 13eleven15? I was well aware that this would be totally unacceptable for most of our members. Indeed, the very fact that I was meeting him might generate negative reactions. So I asked one of the group's founding members, Aurélia Gilbert, to come with me. A survivor of the Bataclan attack, Aurélia had herself previously met with mothers of jihadists, including the mother of Foued Mohamed-Aggad, who, alongside Samy Amimour, was a member of the squad that attacked the concert hall.

We arranged to meet Azdyne Amimour in a café on the Place de la Bastille, in central Paris, on 27 February 2017. He did not ask us any questions, but instead gave us a long account of his own story and that of his son, of his journey to Syria and of how they had been reunited. I gave him some advice, in particular suggesting that he make contact with some groups for the parents of jihadis: *Syrien ne bouge agissons* ('Action on Syria'), set up by Dominique Bons, who lost her son in Syria, and SAVE Belgium, a Belgian group founded by Saliha Ben Ali, whose life fell apart when her son Sabri left for Syria in 2013.[2] Our meeting moved me deeply, as Azdyne is an endearing character with a remarkable life story, who gives an immediate impression of humanity, of a great love of life, of tolerance and of self-taught culture. We kept in touch afterwards and exchanged bits of news and messages of sympathy from time to time.

When, in September 2018, the idea of producing a book based on conversations between Azdyne and myself was put forward by the researcher Sébastien Boussois, I was at first a little reluctant.[3] On an almost daily basis, I am accused on social media of being everything from a naïve promoter of wishy-washy liberalism and political correctness, to an

---

2 Saliha Ben Ali has told her story in her book, *Maman, entends-tu le vent? Daech m'a volé mon fils*, L'Archipel, 2018.

3 Sébastien Boussois is a researcher at the Université Libre de Bruxelles in Brussels and the Université du Québec in Montreal. He acts as an advisor to a number of programmes and organisations combatting radicalisation and extremism, and is a specialist on terrorism-related issues who has written numerous studies on the Arab world.

appeaser seeking the moral disarmament of the West, to an Islamo-leftist and an accomplice of Islamism ... I could go on. I also know that many victims who make no such accusations against me are nevertheless not prepared to enter into dialogue with the parents of terrorists. When, during the second trial of Abdelkader Merah, Mohammed Merah's brother, the defendant's mother gave her evidence to the court, the psychologist and director of the victims' support group *Paris Aide aux Victimes* ('Paris Victims' Support'), Carole Damiani, declared that '[The plaintiffs] understand full well what a mother's pain is, but for them, their pain is of a different nature, and it's difficult to hear her saying that she supports her children. For some victims, it's as if their pain was becoming connected: they're saying "I'm suffering", and it's very hard to hear that the mother of the criminals is also suffering.'[4] Azdyne Amimour does not 'support' his son, as Mohammed Merah's mother does, and he in no way condones his actions. Nevertheless, reading Azdyne's words next to mine could be questionable for some victims. How would people react to a dialogue between the fathers of a victim and her killer? Or of a direct accomplice in her murder, as I don't know which of the three attackers fired the bullet that killed Lola – but that makes no difference.

Deep down, why should I refuse to engage in such a dialogue? Ever since 13 November 2015, I have worked to break down simplistic prejudice. And in this particular case I had

4   Carole Damiani, France Inter, 25 March 2019.

absolutely no reason to blame the father for his son's crimes, as I had already got to know Azdyne sufficiently well to see that he had no truck with terrorism or Islamism.

But simply having no reason to refuse was not enough; if I were going to get involved in this project, I would need to be motivated by real objectives. For me, these would be both personal and political. On a personal level, I wanted to understand the reasons that had driven these youngsters, who were the same age as my daughter, to commit this terrible atrocity. I needed to untangle the strings of the puppets who acted out this blood-soaked tragedy, in the hope, vain perhaps, of overcoming the sense of absurdity I felt, and continue to feel, regarding the circumstances of Lola's death. By entering more deeply into dialogue with Samy Amimour's father, I hoped to move forward in this quest. Alongside this, on a political level, this unexpected conversation with a tolerant Muslim man, who was nevertheless the father of a jihadist, presented an extraordinary opportunity to show that we are able to talk to each other. If such an exchange could take place between us, then we could bring down the walls of mistrust, of incomprehension, and sometimes of sheer hatred, which divide our societies.

To my mind, building solidarity and fostering dialogue with the Muslim community is absolutely crucial, and there is nothing naïve whatsoever about this position. It has been said by certain politicians that we are engaged in a 'war on terrorism'. They no doubt expect to reap electoral benefits by using such militaristic language, but it is no less misleading for that: jihadist terrorism, like all forms of terrorism in fact, has no 'military' objective. Its success is measured purely on its ability to provoke clumsy and excessive reactions: clampdowns on freedoms, indiscriminate repression, the manufacturing of heroes and martyrs ... up to and including an eventual war of religion pitting Muslims against non-Muslims worldwide. Similar spirals of violence have happened in the past – during the Algerian war of independence, for example – and it would be madness to commit the same errors again, particularly in a country that is home to several million Muslims, the vast majority of whom hold French nationality. Those who are naïve are in fact the people who think they can 'send them back where they came from' or coerce them into submission.

While I believe that it is essential to reach out to our Muslim compatriots, guests and neighbours, I do not wish to reduce the dialogue contained in this book to a symbolic gesture. I am not conversing with 'a Muslim', but with Azdyne Amimour. Azdyne can no more be reduced to his 'status' as a Muslim as I can be to my status as an atheist with Christian roots. What we are above all else is two fathers who have each lost a child; two people with a love of travel and culture who were both born on the shores of the Mediterranean; two human beings.

*

Azdyne Amimour (AA): Over these past few years, I have met many other parents of jihadists, but also a great number of people affected by the attacks of 13 November 2015, both survivors and victims' loved ones, like Georges Salines. I contacted him after seeing his appearances in the media; I saw it as a way of helping, and it wasn't easy for either of us. I wanted to help in the name of the Islam I believe in, which has nothing to do with the one used by my son as a tool to achieve his appalling ends. I condemn violence in the strongest possible terms, and I condemn my son's actions.

Why write this book? I believe that it was a form of therapy for both of us. Following the attacks, I was seized by an insatiable urge to devour every book written by the families of jihadists. I wanted to understand, to find answers from other people, before I in turn felt the need to speak, to describe the path followed by my son and my own journey to Syria to find him. In doing so I hope to lift the veil of mystery that covers radicalisation and give the lie to the old adage 'like father, like son', or 'like mother, like son'.

Through this dialogue with Georges Salines, I have sought to break down hatred and share the pain of the parents of victims. What unites the two of us today is, more than anything else, a story of trust and friendship. We have grown to like each other as we have tried to understand what happened and prevent it in the future. Together, we have gone back in time, piecing together the stories of our own lives and those of our children. To ensure that such horror never happens again.

1

The Radicalisation of a Son

AA: On 13 November 2015, it had already been several months since I had heard anything from my son Samy. He had left for Syria in September 2013 and by the end he had cut off all contact, most likely as a way of preparing himself. I believe that, from his point of view, we were a lost cause, and he had understood that he wouldn't be able to change our minds. As he saw things, we were bad Muslims, probably irredeemable, and he most likely felt he had nothing more to lose.

On the evening of 13 November, I was in Liège, in Belgium, in the small apartment where I lived behind the clothes shop which I was running. That evening, I shut up the shop relatively early so that I could settle down to watch the football match between France and Germany, which was starting at 8.30pm at the Stade de France in Paris. I got my dinner ready and began watching the match, thinking how I would have liked to have had my son Samy beside me. For a friendly match like this, Samy would have been supporting France for sure, even though we did occasionally support Algeria. In the second half, I saw Patrice Evra play the ball, then hesitate, which wasn't like him. The sound on my tablet wasn't that good, but I could still clearly hear the explosions. At the time, like everyone else, I didn't understand what was going on, but I subsequently learned that the president, François Hollande, had left the stadium. Although all the gates were now locked, the players carried on with the match until the end. Like millions of people watching at home, I didn't realise what had happened straight away. I didn't listen to the news on the radio until later.

GS: Was that when you found out about people being shot on restaurant terraces in Paris and the attack on the Bataclan?

AA: That's right. I contacted my wife Mouna, who was in our family apartment in Drancy, on the northeastern outskirts of Paris, because I knew that our youngest daughter was out with her friends that evening. I asked my wife whether our little girl was OK and whether she had been . . . at the Bataclan. Throughout the rest of the weekend, I listened to the news on the radio a lot. François Hollande announced that searches would be carried out to track down the attackers' accomplices. At that time, nothing was being said officially about the number of terrorists involved or, of course, their identities. On the Sunday, as usual, I came back to Paris. On the way back, I thought again about François Hollande's announcement. With Samy being in Syria, and given the previous raids on our home, I wondered if the police might come back again. Back in our apartment in

Drancy, I got up several times during the night to peek out of the window through a crack in the curtains. This was the night of Sunday 15 November.

And you, Georges, what were you doing on 13 November 2015?

GS: 13 November was a Friday, a day when the feeling of tiredness from the week mingles with the satisfaction of knowing the weekend is coming. It was Friday the 13th, but I didn't care as I'm not superstitious, and what happened that day has done nothing to change this. I broke up my working day with a swim during my lunch hour at the Butte-aux-Cailles swimming pool, in southeast Paris. I used to go there from time to time, and would sometimes meet up for a swim with my daughter Lola. That was what happened that day: she had come with her friend Manon, who worked in the same offices at the publishers Gründ, where both young women were editors. Her mother, Emmanuelle and I saw Lola almost every weekend. I would also sometimes take her out to lunch, now that her publishing company had moved its offices to the Place d'Italie – where we are talking today – which is just a few hundred yards from my own offices.

I didn't spend long in the pool that day, as I'd forgotten my swimming goggles. Lola and I chatted about nothing in particular. When you don't have any reason to think that you won't see each other again, you don't say the things that really matter. She said that she would come round to our house for lunch the next day. I didn't know that there would be no tomorrow for her, and that this would be our last conversation. I didn't ask her what she would be doing that evening, either.

AA: So you didn't know that she was going to the Bataclan?

GS: No. I only found out later on that she had been invited to the Eagles of Death Metal concert by a friend who had an extra ticket. That evening, her friend was hit in the buttocks by one bullet, while Lola was hit by two, one of which killed her.

AA: I will always wonder why it was that day, that band, that place ...

GS: So much idiotic nonsense has been spouted on this subject. Some ill-informed people have claimed that the band's songs contain satanic lyrics, and that their name has some sinister meaning. In actual fact, their name is a play on words which came out of a quip made by their lead singer. When a journalist once asked him if their music was death metal, he had replied: 'If what we do is death metal, then we're the Eagles of death metal', the joke being that whereas death metal is a pretty extreme music genre, the Eagles were a group whose sound is often considered by rock fans to be overly staid and sophisticated. So the name of the band was nothing more than a knowing wink to rock culture.

AA: Did Lola like that type of music?

GS: Lola liked heavy metal and hard rock, although she preferred more melodic and complex sounds like Arcade Fire or David Bowie. She went a few times to Hellfest, the Mecca for metalheads held in Clisson, on the French Atlantic coast. So I'm not surprised at all that she decided to go to the Bataclan to listen to the Eagles of Death Metal.

AA: Tell me something about Lola, other than all the things that I've already read in the media since that terrible day.

GS: She shared a flat in the eastern 20th *arrondissement* of Paris with another girl, Agathe ... and their cat Billy who they were both very fond of! That summer, Billy had fallen from the fifth-floor balcony, so Lola had decided not to go on a planned trip to India. Instead, she spent some of the summer relaxing with her brothers in Montpellier, where her cousin lives. I know that she had a wonderful time during those holidays. She had just begun a relationship with a young man, the coach of her roller derby team. She was mad about this sport, which suited her to a tee: joyous, playful, rebellious, team-oriented, unconventional.

It was also a period of intense work-related activity for her, as she was in the process of launching a new publishing brand, 404 Editions, which she had created and named after the 'error 404' message that comes up when a web page can't be found. The books published under this brand were aimed at a 'geeky' readership and she had even come up with a slogan: '*The page you no longer need to search for*'. All in all, I think that 2015 was the year of her greatest-ever challenges. This was a tragedy, because she wouldn't have the time to see them through; but in another way maybe it was a good thing, because she left on a high note, in a period of excitement and happiness.

Identity and religion

GS: Azdyne, can you try to tell me what could have led to Samy's involvement in the atrocity at the Bataclan? Do you remember the first time that he showed any interest in religion and in Islam?

AA: Yes, it dates back to when he was about fifteen, in 2003, and it happened in an insidious manner, I would say. One day, his mother, Mouna, took him to see the doctor. After the consultation, the doctor took my wife to one side for a word; he explained that he had been intrigued by something that Samy had told him. My son, it turned out, had said that he felt uncomfortable with the fact that his parents, as Muslims, did not pray. It was true that neither my wife nor I prayed, and Mouna doesn't cover her hair.

That same year, Samy went on holiday to Senegal with his uncle and aunt. When he was over there, he learned how to fish and shoot pigeons, which he enjoyed. In spite of this, he hadn't seemed very enthusiastic about his holiday, maybe because it was the first time he had been a long way away from his mother.

The year he turned fifteen was not a happy one in any case, as this was when his cousin Roxane killed herself. He didn't see her very often, but I think that losing her had a big effect on him. It was his first experience of death, and from then on he began praying.

GS: Did you notice this change immediately?

AA: Some of his friends mentioned it to me, but I also

picked up on some things that seemed to bother him about my attitude to religion. For instance, in 2006, I was running a bar in central Paris, Le Cléopâtre, in the Bastille district. One Saturday, I invited the whole family to have lunch there. As usual, Samy was keeping himself to himself, and when I brought out a beer, I got a very clear feeling that he was uncomfortable. I thought that I could even see a kind of hatred in his eyes.

GS: Maybe he was beginning to experience difficulties related to 'identity-construction', as people say today. In any case, how do your children define themselves? What do they consider themselves to be first and foremost? French? Algerian? Muslim?

AA: Samy and his two sisters are French and Algerian, and it's not something that has ever really raised any serious questions. When the children were little, we used to spend our holidays in Algeria and Tunisia. I tried to give them some Arabic lessons, particularly to Samy, who showed a glimmer of interest, unlike my two daughters, who couldn't see any point in it.

GS: They say that sometimes, when you come from two cultures, in reality you belong to none. This feeling of belonging or of non-belonging is often complex and seems to plunge some people into utter despair.

AA: We need to build bridges from one shore of the Mediterranean to the other in order to close this huge chasm that our children have to live with. That's what we were trying to do during our summer holidays. We would go to Lorraine in eastern France to see the children's maternal grandparents, and to Annaba in Algeria to visit my family, particularly my brothers and sisters. From Algeria, we'd go on to Tunisia, near Tabarka, where the beaches are nice. At the end of the day, I don't know whether Samy considered himself more French or more Algerian: I think he tended to just give in to one or other of his origins.

GS: 'Give in' – that's an odd expression ... It's quite unlike, say, 'discover himself'.

AA: I don't think it was necessarily a conscious decision. Samy seemed to like spending time in Lorraine with his maternal grandparents, and he would come back full of joy. In Algeria he had dozens of cousins to play with, as I've got fourteen brothers and sisters. Everyone liked him: they called him 'Oui' because he said yes to everything. Although he was shy, he liked to hang out with a group; it must have reassured him. Once, with his mates, he went and let down the tyres on several cars. I didn't approve, of course, but in a way I was pleased that he had taken a risk, that he had done something a bit daring.

GS: You do realise all the same that it was 'slightly' illegal and punishable by the law?

AA: Yes, of course, but it never happened again. His mother was very worried – to tell the truth she was always worried about him – whereas I didn't think that it was a huge cause for concern. When she kept on about it, I even said to her: 'Come on, let him be, he hasn't killed anyone!'

GS: Ah ...

AA: Perhaps I should have given Samy a couple of good slaps when he was a child . . . But I never hit him. Even when he was in Syria, I always listened to him without contradicting him, without daring to.

I did shake him around a couple of times, like the time in Algeria when I gave him a good telling off on the beach because he'd disappeared for several hours with his cousin. I'd been terrified because, the previous summer, I'd saved two children from drowning, and I still had those images in my head. That evening, I didn't feel good at all, I'd been so frightened of losing him.

Was I too soft on him? I don't know. He was a good boy and for a long time I thought that he was happy. We were very open-minded. We even had a Christmas tree! My thinking was that, since we were in France, and a lot of his friends were celebrating Christmas, I didn't want him to miss out. Sometimes I even dressed up as Father Christmas to bring the presents! The children would be sitting nicely under the tree with their stockings.

GS: That's unusual for a Muslim family, isn't it? You know, my wife and I never bothered keeping up the whole Christmas myth with our children. I didn't raise them to believe in Father Christmas.

AA: I can't be accused of having been intolerant . . . The miracles of the Prophet and of Jesus, the three wise men, the healing of the sick, Christ's tragic death – they have always fascinated me. But you on the other hand were a bit hard on your children!

GS: I think that I never wanted to present stories to my children as being true when I didn't believe in them myself. All the same, the children loved Christmas, with the meal and the presents. I told them Christmas stories, but I always told them that Father Christmas was an imaginary character. They knew that the presents came from their parents.

AA: For me, it was a way of introducing my children to the culture of the country they were living in. I always left them the choice. The same went for Ramadan; we never forced our children to practise it with us. None of them would pray during the rest of the year, any more than we did ourselves to tell the truth. I was a believer but not a practising Muslim. Nevertheless, like for all Algerians, Ramadan was a family and cultural ritual that we had to follow.

GS: Personally, I think I wanted above all for my children to be able to trust what I told them completely. You say that you're a believer; I'm not, but I'm always curious to know about other people's beliefs. Why do you believe? Who is God, for you?

AA: I believe in a God who is the great architect of the universe and I believe in the Prophet who was sent to us. This God is also within me and I know that He is keeping a tally of my good and bad actions. When the children were small, I didn't talk much about religion, I just explained the basics of Islam to them. It was Samy who, later on, brought me back to religion and prayer.

From prayer to radicalisation

GS: Was there any particular moment when you feared that Samy was going off the rails?

AA: On our visits to Algeria in the summer, particularly during the dark years of the 1990s, I saw evidence of the madness that could lead some Muslims to commit the most terrible acts. When I noticed that Samy was becoming interested in religion, I decided to get on the front foot, and in 2008, when he was twenty-one, I suggested that he could enquire about studying theology in Brussels at the Université libre de Bruxelles and becoming an imam. I would have preferred him to have been able to profess his religion in a healthy and peaceful way after receiving training at a public institution from qualified staff rather than falling under malign influences.

GS: What had his sources of information on Islam been up until then? What had he read?

AA: I know that when he was twenty-four, in 2011, when he was beginning to become radicalised, he read the Koran in the translation by the Islamic scholar Tariq Ramadan. He was also following a certain 'Abourayan' in Belgium through the internet. He even suggested that I should watch the videos produced by this man, whose words he found inspiring. It turns out that this Abourayan character, as I would later discover, had links to Sharia4Belgium, the jihadist recruiting organisation in Antwerp led by Fouad Belkacem. Abourayan, or Michael

Debreda to give him his real name, was a convert. Was there a link? In any case, Samy would talk to me more and more about his new-found friends in Brussels, but I don't think he ever went there.

GS: Do you think that Samy's journey down the wrong path began with this individual?

AA: Maybe. Unfortunately, though, Abourayan wasn't the only one Samy came across. He was also very keen on material posted on the internet by a Turk named Harun Yahya, who was subsequently arrested. Harun Yahya lived in a large villa surrounded by women, and was part of the Islamic creationist movement, whose doctrine is akin to evangelical Christianity. The movement is opposed to Darwinist evolution, and propounds the theory that everything was made by God's hand. Yahya was a promoter of anti-Zionism, anti-Masonism and a homophobe, and participated actively in public debate until he was arrested for fraud and sexual assault. His writings continue to circulate around the world. My friend Saliha Ben Ali, the mother of a jihadist and the founder of the charity SAVE Belgium, was recently sent some of his books . . .

As well as these internet videos, Samy read a whole series of religious books, some of the titles of which I found suspicious. These included: *I Want to Repent But . . .*, *How To Build Your Faith*, *Yes! I Converted to Islam*, *A Muslim Woman in a French Family*, *The Signs of the End Times*, etc. One day, he even presented his mother with a French translation of the Koran.

GS: *The Signs of the End Times* ... that sends a shiver down my spine. You can find that sort of literature in Salafist bookshops all over Europe, but it seems like, at this stage, it was all just theoretical for Samy. Was there a catalyst? The Arab Spring in 2011 and the war in Syria?

AA: At the beginning, he didn't really have an opinion on any of those questions. I'm sure that it took someone else to lead him on and sow the seeds of revolt and hatred. At that time he was also in a period of transition in his career. He'd not only dropped out of a law degree at university, but also stopped studying for his technical diploma in transport. After doing a few temporary jobs at the council offices and elsewhere, he got an internship with the RATP, the Parisian public transport company. My wife and I felt relieved, especially when he was later taken on as a bus driver on the 148 Bobigny–Le Blanc-Mesnil route. He would stick with it for a year. I'd dreamt of great things for him and had suggested that he study law to become a solicitor but, seeing how things were, I thought it best to take a pragmatic line. In truth, we were a long way from suspecting that he was actually working in order to save money up to go to Syria ...

GS: Did you let him know how disappointed you were regarding his life choices?

AA: I kept my annoyance to myself, but inside I was fuming: 'Right, so I've spent my whole life working my fingers to the bone just so you can become a bus driver?!' One day, almost as if he'd heard me despite my silence, and probably feeling that he was being judged, he yelled at me: 'If your business isn't doing well, Dad, it's because you don't pray enough.' That was like a punch in the gut. I had the feeling that the harder we tried to find solutions for him, the worse things were getting. At that moment, I realised that he was really beginning to go off the rails.

The wrong company

AA: I think that, to begin with, going back to Islam was a way for Samy to turn his life around and gain a sense of identity. Having not connected that strongly with a French or Algerian identity, for the first time in his life he was becoming proud of an identity that he was able to choose and, above all, construct with a view to attaining fixed objectives. Identity can't just be something you inherit; it also has to hold promise for the future. And we could see it happening, my wife and I: he began exercising, working out, looking at himself regularly in the mirror, growing to like himself, then love himself. All the ingredients of his downfall were there: a crisis of identity, a series of setbacks, his thirst for knowledge regarding Islam, his easily led nature ... All that, along with falling into the wrong company.

GS: The wrong company ... at the wrong time. Saliha Ben Ali has talked about how her son 'began listening to the declarations of Fouad Belkacem, the leader of Sharia4Belgium (subsequently imprisoned and stripped of his

Belgian nationality), who said: 'You're not Belgians, you're not Moroccans. You're above any nationality because you're Muslims. And Muslims are superior to all other peoples.'[5]

AA: For us, as parents, it was hard to know who Samy was really seeing. We had one neighbour, from Djerba in Tunisia, whom I paid no attention to at first, but who probably encouraged Samy in his rediscovery of Islam and the vision of the world that it would give him. It all came back to me subsequently: after 11 September 2001, from one day to the next, this guy from Djerba began letting his beard grow. He was only seventeen or eighteen, just a kid. Several times, he came knocking on our door to talk about Islam. I asked him what he thought he could teach me about my religion, seeing as I was the same age as his father. He wanted to talk to us about the Prophet, about prayer, about the obligations of being a Muslim, and every time would recite a speech he had learned by heart in broken Arabic. Mouna and I would block the doorway, but he kept coming back like a leech. Did Samy end up listening to him? I'll never know, as he's left since. And yet on the same floor there was our neighbour Richard, who was Jewish and had always been extremely open-minded. As an Arab who grew up in the 1960s, meeting him was a shock to my ingrained beliefs about Jews!

It was only later on that I would work out that it was Samy's closest friends, especially the ones who went with him to Syria, who were the real trigger: it was a form of

---

5   *Cahiers de l'Orient* n° 134, 2019/2, 'Quelle contre-radicalisation?'.

generational solidarity for them, with their shared frustrations, a project which in their eyes promised salvation ...

GS: How long did Samy stay with the RATP?

AA: For a long time, we were under the impression that after a few months he had taken a year's sabbatical leave. We were wrong. I had said to myself at the time that the RATP wouldn't have paid to train him and then just let him go on leave a few months later; it didn't make any sense. Of course, he didn't tell us anything during this period: this was an example of the famous *taqiya*, the art of hiding one's real intentions ... In fact, he had resigned from his job and was getting ready to go to Syria. At the same time, he also began attending various mosques regularly, going around at night to help poor people in the neighbourhood, and sending big bags of clothes to people in Syria. To my mind, this was the first link he established with Syria.

GS: Which mosque did he pray in? Was it in Drancy, where the famous imam Hassen Chalghoumi preaches? He keeps a high profile in the media, although he's also widely criticised for his unorthodox positions.

AA: No, and perhaps for those exact reasons. Chalghoumi isn't the strictest of imams, and he openly proclaims his right-wing political views and liking for conservative former president Nicolas Sarkozy. Samy did, however, attend the mosque at Blanc-Mesnil in the northeastern suburbs, which was the target of some attention from the security services for a while, and was apparently considered by some media sources to be Salafist. After the Bataclan attack, the Muslim cultural association of Blanc-Mesnil nevertheless put out a press release stating that Samy had never belonged to the mosque's congregation.

GS: But did you ever go there with him?

AA: I went there with him once, during Ramadan in 2012. He was wearing a *qamis* and didn't speak to me at all on the journey there.[6] Once we were inside, he went over to a group of friends and introduced me to them, before beginning to pray. I felt very out of place. I went to the back of the mosque and said my own prayers. The imam arrived and preached his sermon. I didn't hear anything that shocked or scandalised me. Then Samy disappeared with his friends and I was left alone with all the sorrow of the world in my heart. We had grown so far apart over those last years ... I just didn't know what to do. His daily routine seemed to be firmly set: he would wake up at 4.00am, set off to the mosque by car or on foot with his friends – sometimes he went to the one in Le Bourget, near Drancy – then he would stay there for hours in the evening after its doors had closed. What was going on inside? I haven't the faintest idea.

GS: Do you think that he was radicalised at the mosque?

AA: We'll only ever be able to speculate. We did hear rumours that there was a hard core of Salafists within the RATP; he may have got involved with them. At one point I thought that he had left the company to get closer to them,

---

6 Translator's note: the *qamis* is the long robe traditionally worn by men in the Gulf region.

but there were also other, more troubling signs. We found out that he had enrolled in a shooting club on the Rue de la Reine-Blanche in southern Paris. And it wasn't just any club – it was run by the National Police, although in principle anyone can join. If you're sponsored by an existing member, or by a police officer, you can join the club as long as you have a clean criminal record, and can produce a medical certificate stating that you are fit to participate in physical activity and target sports, along with a copy of your identity card. At the time, we couldn't see why he would need to learn how to handle a weapon. It was only later that we found out that his childhood friend, Charaf, had joined a year earlier; but I don't know how they managed to get sponsorship for their applications. It was also around this time that Samy met his future wife, Kahina, probably while he was driving his bus route with the RATP. She was from Blanc-Mesnil and she would follow him to Syria at the beginning of 2015, where they got married. You've got to laugh, wearing the *burqa* when you're called Kahina . . .

GS: Why?

AA: Well, you see, Kahina was a great Berber queen, of Jewish faith, who at the end of the seventh century fought against the Arab invaders . . . who were Muslims!

GS: You couldn't make it up! I suppose that Samy's journey to Syria was planned as part of a wider scheme: to move away, fight, get married, have children, turn his life around . . . Had he given anything away about all this? Were you aware of any other plans to move away or travel?

AA: The subject did come up more and more often in 2012. Samy was already twenty-five, so it was difficult to exert much influence over him. He started to talk to me about going to Afghanistan 'to learn Arabic'. I gave a start and replied that it was an absurd idea, given that they don't speak Arabic in Afghanistan! I could see that he didn't have a clue what he was talking about and that the idea wasn't actually his. The time after that, he spoke about a plan to go to Yemen, again for the same reason. To discourage him, I told him that it wasn't the ideal place and that he wouldn't like the heat and the poverty. He was unstable and I suspected that he would change his mind. I didn't mention anything to my wife, but I knew that Al Qaeda had a presence in Yemen. So I tried to steer him towards Algeria, where he could learn Arabic perfectly well, but without any success ... He came back later with the idea of Egypt. I was torn: I was worried, but at the same time pleased that he would at last be learning the language of his origins, particularly since he would be studying at the prestigious Al-Azhar University in Cairo.

The descent into hell

GS: When did Samy begin having problems with the law?

AA: By this time, he was only ever wearing the *qamis*, and he had given all his 'European' outfits to me. He was hanging around with two childhood friends from Drancy, Samir and Charaf. One day, one of them let a person who was listed as a terror suspect stay in his flat, and that marked the beginning of the descent into hell. They began planning to go to Syria and join the *jihad*. I think that Charaf, who was the oldest of the three, was probably the ringleader, and the two others just went along with him. At the time, Mouna and I didn't notice any of this. Secretive, shy and withdrawn, Samy was the perfect candidate for Daesh.

GS: Were Samir and Charaf involved in any criminal activities?

AA: Not at all, none of the three were. So the first police raid on our apartment came like a bolt from the blue.

GS: What happened? Were you at home?

AA: Yes, at the time I was shuttling between Paris and Belgium for my clothes business, but on 16 October 2012 I was in the apartment at Drancy. It was still dark at around 7.00am, when I heard the sound of the heavy brigade arriving, a confused din of rushing feet, clanking metal and voices which woke me from my sleep. If they had rung the bell, I would have let them in, but before I had time to even think, the front door was smashed in. My first thought was that it was burglars, until I saw masked men storming into the apartment. 'Don't move!' one of them yelled, pointing his gun at me. My wife and I were immediately handcuffed and moved to the kitchen. They seemed to know exactly what they were looking for and where Samy's bedroom was. He was also brought out in handcuffs, and when he came near us, he looked frightened to see my wife and me chained up, back to back. I asked what was going on and he said: 'I swear, Dad, I haven't done anything wrong.' I asked one of the policemen whether it was to do with drugs. He just replied: 'Drugs? No, no.' Then they put a hood over his head and took him away. Samy spent four days under arrest, during which time everything you can imagine went through our heads.

GS: What did you do during those days, which must have seemed neverending?

AA: I had to go to Liège to open the clothes shop which I had just set up. Mouna was in a panic, but I reassured her over the telephone, saying they might have got Samy mixed up with someone else ... We would soon learn that Charaf and Samir had also been arrested.

GS: How were things after he was released?

AA: When Samy came home, he was weak because he hadn't eaten anything, as the meals weren't *halal*. I was in Belgium and we talked a bit over the phone. He told me that, during the raid, he had been frightened of being shot through the window if he tried to escape. When I got back, he took us out to dinner to explain what had happened: 'Charaf let one of his friends, who's a terror suspect, stay with him. The police must have seen that we were friends, that's all.' My wife and I exchanged dubious glances, but what could we do? Samy was twenty-five; we had no way of forcing him to reveal the truth to us.

GS: Today, do you know what they were accused of in 2012?

AA: Yes, but finding out took some doing. We haven't been able to access all the documents in his file, but after they were released from custody, they were investigated for conspiracy to engage in acts of terrorism. The famous anti-terrorist prosecutor Marc Trévidic assembled the case against them. The police had tapped their phones and discovered that the three of them wanted to go to Yemen, not to learn Arabic, obviously, but to take part in *jihad*. Samy was questioned by David Bénichou, the other prosecutor working on the case, while Charaf and Samir were questioned by Marc Trévidic. The established facts were that the three of them had searched the internet about how to get to the Pakistan–Afghanistan region; one of them had even requested a visa to enter Pakistan. Then, Charaf had let a certain M'Bodji stay in his home, who was listed as a terror suspect because he had spent time in Yemen. Since getting into Pakistan seemed too complicated, they fell back on the plan to go to Yemen. In the meantime, M'Bodji had gone to Djibouti, and the three others tried with difficulty to put their plans into action. Samy made enquiries with travel agencies about passing through Oman, and I later learned from a journalist that, between them, Charaf and Samir had put aside 20,000 euros. I'll never know how much Samy had saved up for his 'great journey', but under the pretext of a holiday with friends in the south of France, he had bought camping equipment (sleeping bags, walking boots, etc. . . .). Suspecting that their departure was imminent, the police had launched the raid. There was no way we could have imagined what was going on. I would later hear from a source that they had wanted to arrest them before they left for Yemen. Their case was brought to court and the three of them were placed on probation. At this point, Charaf sent word to M'Bodji that their attempt to leave the country had failed, and made a new plan to go to Tataouine, in Tunisia, to join a group of Salafist extremists. M'Bodji was eventually found in Mali, from where, it turns out, he would later contact Samy.

GS: This whole episode sounds more like something from the Keystone Cops than a real commando operation! But I suppose that once they were on the ground, the apprentice jihadists would become more 'professional'.

AA: Especially seeing as their brush with the law didn't shake them up. Worse still, the three of them were supposed to check in with the authorities, and this time it was the state that went about things in an amateurish manner. The justice system eventually realised that all of them had stopped checking in with the local police station. I would later learn from a friend who's a lawyer that, under civil law, there is no way for judges to confirm whether a person on probation is still checking in.

GS: This was before 2015, and I think the system has been tightened up considerably since. Let's hope so, anyway.

AA: Yes, there were failures, there's no doubt about it, since Samy, Charaf and Samir ended up going to Syria in September 2013, just when the country was beginning to become the destination of choice for jihadists. All three of them were forbidden from leaving the country at the time, and had had their identity papers confiscated. But we later learned that Samy had gone to the police station to declare that his identity card had been stolen, then requested a new one from the town hall, and that a new card was issued to him from the regional offices at Bobigny! How was it possible that no administrative checks were in place? After the attacks, we were assured that checks had been made. But it so happens that, from the voluntary work that she does alongside employees at the town hall, Mouna actually knew the worker who handed Samy his identity card. He confirmed that my son had come to pick up his card in person. Unfortunately, this isn't the only murky detail in this affair ... What I know for sure is, at this time, there was no interface between the list of wanted persons and the list of confiscated papers belonging to people on probation. This is how Samy and his accomplices would leave France and travel to Syria, which was a more accessible destination than Afghanistan or Yemen. As the war was picking up in intensity at this time, their judgement was correct.

GS: As a proportion of the number of people who left for Syria, few jihadists came back to commit attacks in France, which is very fortunate. It's already quite incredible that, despite having been designated as terror suspects, put before a court and placed on probation, they should have been able to leave the country; but to then be let back into France with no questions asked ... The Schengen Area really is a leaky sieve! Or at least it was at that time.

Syria, the point of no return

GS: In practical terms, how did Samy, Charaf and Samir organise their departure?

AA: I know that Charaf went over to Syria before the others. I think that he acted as a middleman to bring over the other two, after having himself been recruited by M'Bodji. A few weeks before he left, Samy bought a car with his savings. I know that he waited a long time to get it registered in his name and insured; we didn't understand why. A few days before, he gave a lot of his old clothes to his mother, and took some others away, we supposed in order to give them out to the poor during his nightly rounds. And then Tuesday 3 September 2013 came. That morning, Samy came and kissed me and hugged me tight. I was off to Liège the same day and found it a bit strange, as we weren't really that tactile with each other. During my journey, I couldn't stop thinking about this gesture, and once I got to Liège I called my wife. She told me she was sure I was worrying about nothing, but I wasn't wrong. Later, Mouna would think back to how Samy had – or rather hadn't – looked at her when he went out of the front door to the lift. He hadn't turned around because, as he later admitted to his sister, a last look back towards his mother might have made him change his mind.

GS: It's so terrifying, this departure with no possibility of return. He couldn't go back to his parents. It was as if he were about to lose every last vestige of innocence, every hope of redemption. And nothing would ever be the same again.

AA: Yes, Georges, that was the moment I lost my son for the first time. He was sighted in Turkey on 6 September 2013. I imagine that they got there by car. He called his mother on Skype shortly afterwards to announce that he was in Syria: 'Don't come looking for me. I'm with Charaf and Samir. Everything's fine.' When I called him, I tried to get angry, demanding that he come home, but I was worried that if I put his back up, he'd just disappear completely. We didn't have any hold over him. I now know that he immediately joined the al-Nusra Front in al-Sham, as Syria is sometimes called, but we had no information and thought that he might have joined a humanitarian organisation.

GS: I can imagine how difficult it must be to know what to do. I'm sure I would have found myself facing the same dilemma as you did: getting angry or trying to remain calm and reasoning with him in the hope that he might go back on his decision.

AA: He explained that he wasn't going to the front line, that he was helping the local population and learning Arabic. He never told us that he had gone out to take part in *jihad*. Subsequently, though, our Skype conversations left no doubt in our minds as to what was going on: one day, we could clearly see Kalashnikovs behind him, in a completely empty room. When I asked him about this, he replied that the guns belonged to other clients in the internet café.

GS: By staying in contact with you, was he trying to re-assure you or convince you that what he was doing was right?

AA: He called us every week, on Sunday, which was the

day I would come back home. At the beginning, he talked to us about his humanitarian work helping Syrians who were suffering under Bashar al-Assad's regime. Then, gradually, he changed tack and began trying to convince us to join him, a classic method of indoctrination. 'Come and see, I've got cats here, a big house, a swimming pool ... Why are you staying in Europe?!' he'd often tell us. He even developed a far closer relationship via Skype with his sisters Alya and Maïssa than he ever had when he was living with them. It was really surprising.

GS: Did you try to warn the police? To get help from a lawyer?

AA: No, we were too scared that he would cut off all contact. Realising that you no longer trust your child is a complicated thing for parents. And this was in 2013, before Daesh existed, and things weren't so clear-cut. There was no helpline to call, for instance. That was only set up in 2014.[7]

The last-ditch journey

GS: You tried to go and find him in Syria, didn't you? That was a risky journey ...

AA: Yes, I decided to go there. On 13 June 2014, nine months after Samy left, I set off from Belgium to Turkey.

---

7 The Inter-Ministerial Committee for the Prevention of Crime and Radicalisation subsequently created a freephone helpline in France (0800 005 696) for families to call if they are concerned about a young person becoming radicalised.

In my bag I had both my passports – French and Algerian – 400 euros in cash and two mobile phones. I took a flight from Charleroi to Istanbul, then an internal flight to Hatay, in eastern Turkey. I had found out that Samy had also passed through Hatay, a town on the border with Syria. Mouna gave me a letter which she had written for him and then went away for a few days to see our daughter Alya, who lives in Dubai, for some moral support. On arriving in Turkey, I fell ill and spent several days shut away in my hotel room in Hatay. From my window, I could see the border. I knew that the Syrian intelligence services were stepping up their activities, and I was on my guard. In the hotel I began making contacts, passing myself off as a journalist thanks to an old press card that I'd held onto from the time when I used to write a cinema column in the magazine *Paris Loisirs*. I needed at all costs to find a way of getting into Syria without attracting attention.

GS: What did Mouna say in her letter to Samy?

AA: I'll read it to you:

'Hello my son, Every day, I pray for your safety. Every day, my thoughts are with you, from the morning until I go to sleep. I have a wound in the depths of my heart. My flesh, my blood, I will never forget your look when you left. In the depths of my being, I knew it, but I would never have believed that you, who I so cherished, even if you didn't realise how much, would leave me this way. My heart weeps every day and my only wish is for you to be happy, where you have chosen to make your life, even if it is far from me.

I want you to start a family and I ask God to protect you, my beloved son. I miss you so much, and if you tell me every day that you are well, that will be enough for me. I kiss you with all my heart, as do all those who love you. Granny and Grandpa are very upset and pray for you every day. So do your aunt and all your cousins, too! Hugs and kisses, my son. I love you with all my heart. See you soon, *inshallah*. Your mother.'

GS: She doesn't say anything about you, his father ...

AA: No, it's her letter. Maybe it's a bit surprising, but I can understand. The view from Hatay reminded me of the landscapes that I had known in Syria in the 1960s, when I used to visit from Jordan, where I was living. Nothing seemed to have changed. After having regained my strength, I got into a smuggler's taxi which took me to the border. I only wanted to call Samy once I was safely inside Syria, so as to increase my chances of finding him.

GS: Was it easy to get into Syria?

AA: It was quite complicated, actually: only Syrian passport holders were allowed back into their country. Samy had got through in 2013, when the border was still like a sieve. I went back to the hotel and called him, telling him straight out: 'I'm in Turkey, at the Syrian border. I've come to see you.' He was taken aback, and replied in a quite unpleasant tone. He no doubt suspected that I wanted to convince him to come back home. If I mentioned the subject just once, that would be it. He then told me to cross over at Gaziantep, two hundred kilometres away, and call him once I had arrived.

My bet had paid off; he was prepared to lead me to where he was: 'Give me your Turkish number and a guy called Omar will call you to bring you across. Note down his number.'

GS: Did you go to Gaziantep straight away?

AA: Yes, I booked into a hotel and hung around waiting for someone to call me. One day passed, then two, still nothing. I tried to make some contacts myself. On a café terrace, I again passed myself off as a journalist, and I came across two former Islamist fighters who had deserted the front. They advised me against going into Syria, saying that their experience of the country had borne no relation to what they had been promised. A Circassian even offered to go and fetch Samy for me: for 100 euros, he could get him across the border on the back of a donkey! Time seemed to be moving incredibly slowly. On the third day, at 7.00am, there was a knock on the door of my room: 'Are you the person who wants to get into Syria? Get your stuff ready. We're leaving in ten minutes.' He was Turkish and spoke in English. 'Someone will come and get you, not necessarily me. Wait downstairs. He'll recognise you.' I went down to the lobby. Eventually, a man turned up in a manner which made it impossible not to notice him. After flashing me a glance, he went out again and I followed him. We stopped in front of a packed minibus. There were women wearing black *niqabs*, children, and men wearing *qamis*. There was only one free seat: mine.

I was asked why I wanted to go, and I replied that I was going to find my son, who had gone to take part in *jihad*. My interlocutor suddenly seemed to get cold feet: 'We'll call you back.' And the bus left without me. Back to square one, and I was beginning to get seriously annoyed.

Two days later, another man came to see me at the hotel: 'Get your bag ready, somebody will come and get you.' Again, a crammed minibus and the same population wearing veils or *qamis*. Arabs, Tunisians, Moroccans, Turks, Saudis ... From the sound of their voices and accents, I could tell that it was a really very cosmopolitan group. One Saudi who looked about twenty was listening to music and *anashids*, patriotic Daesh chants; he looked really pumped up.

GS: How was it, getting across the border?

AA: We changed car seven or eight times. The first time, I said that I was going to see my son; the second time, Samy must have called them. We got in through the town of Karkamis. I can remember it being unbearably hot, it was 1.00pm and we were opposite a wide plain and a grove of pistachio trees. Our vehicle suddenly stopped: on the track in front of us, three hundred metres away, was a Turkish army tank. We were told to get out of our cars and line up in single file, then we waited for other vehicles to arrive for several hours under the scorching sun. There wasn't a single cloud in the sky and I was quite prepared for anything to happen, including having to turn back.

I finally made it into Syria on 27 June, the first day of Ramadan and two days before the proclamation of the Caliphate by Daesh, on 29 June 2014. In the distance, I could see the first roadblock flying the black flag of Islamic

State. A jihadist wearing a *qamis* and carrying a Kalashnikov came up to us and signalled for us to go through. Then we took another car towards Jarablus, a border town beside the Euphrates. Passing through these landscapes, I had the feeling that I was going back over my own past, but this time with Samy's face in the background. It was quite troubling.

We arrived at a barracks set up in a converted school. The women and children were put on one side, the men on the other. When we went in, we found about thirty bearded men all sitting there on the floor, as if they were waiting for us. For the first time, I felt afraid. They greeted us with shouts of *'Allahu Akbar'* and one of them, even more terrifying than the others, got up, took my head in his hands, and kissed me on the forehead. I thought about saying that I had come to see my son, but I kept quiet, as my age said it all anyway. Our group was greeted with expressions of encouragement and thanks. There was one German, probably a convert, and a lot of Asians, but to tell the truth, with the beards, it was hard to tell where people came from just by looking at them.

GS: Did you speak to anyone?

AA: I struck up a conversation with the one who had kissed me. I got round to talking about my son and asked him whether there were any Algerians in the room. He replied that there were more Moroccans and Tunisians, but told me that a man and his ten-year-old son, sitting next to me, were Algerian. His was a grim story, like so many others: after living in England, the father had joined Daesh, while his

Irish wife along with his seventeen-year-old daughter had been shut away in a *madafa*.[8] As soon as he arrived in Syria, the father had torn up the family's British passports.

GS: How was this 'barracks' organised? I've heard that there was an *emir* in each one.

AA: That's right, later we went to see the *emir*, the local Daesh commander. He was surrounded by a dozen men all armed to the teeth, and was dressed in a *qamis*, with a beard and long hair. When a man explained to him that I had come to see my son, I gave him the *nom de guerre* that Samy had mentioned on the telephone, 'Abu Qital' ('Father of Battle'). 'Which *katiba*[9] is he in?' he asked me. When I gave him the name Samy had told me, he fixed me with his stare and told everyone else to leave the room. I had the feeling that I'd given the wrong name and feared that I'd fallen into the hands of a rival faction. At last, he took me in his arms before saying: 'Your son is in the *katiba* of heroes. You see, the people who are here are undergoing training and all dream of joining this combat unit, the best there is. So stay here and sleep tonight.'

Taking advantage of this unexpected credit which I now enjoyed, I asked to contact Samy. Since there was no network, I was taken by scooter to a phone box, accompanied by an escort with a Kalashnikov slung across his back. Just then, the call to prayer rang out and the street emptied in a

---

8 House for women.
9 Combat unit.

few seconds. It was dusk and the atmosphere felt as if the end of the world had come.

'Samy, I'm in Jarablus.'

'All right, I'll come and get you tomorrow morning,' he replied curtly.

'Fine. Where are you?' There was no reply.

GS: So in the end, Samy did nothing to stop you coming to see him. That was quite a gamble.

AA: Yes. I later found out that he was in Manbij, thirty-eight kilometres from Jarablus. I went back to the barracks, which was a pretty inhospitable place. There was a queue for the toilets and the food was revolting. As for the atmosphere, it was hardly any better – no music, obviously. Sitting around on the floor, people were telling each other about their adventures, why they had joined up, what they hoped to do in Syria. Some were idealists, some were lunatics. I went from one room to another and found groups belonging to different nationalities. 'In spite of your age you still came, well done!' the *emir* said to me with respect. I spent a terrible night and dreamed that Samy had been wounded. This was clearly a premonition ... At five in the morning, the call to prayer rang out. Despite being exhausted, we all got up to pray, while the *emir* stayed in bed!

GS: What was it like seeing Samy again?

AA: I waited until ten in the morning, then saw Samy arriving. He was wearing a paramilitary uniform and walking on crutches with a Kalashnikov slung over his shoulder. He came up to me, smiling. His face was haggard, with a little goatee and his piercing eyes, there he was. He seemed almost possessed, so sure of himself, manly. He looked at least five years older.

He told me that he had been hit by several bullets in the thigh. He was calm, cold, and this wasn't the warm reunion I had been expecting. Then we set off together for Manbij, in a jeep that looked like it had been captured from Bashar al-Assad's army. I was looking at Samy but had trouble finding anything to say to him. In spite of his physical metamorphosis, he was no more talkative than he had been before.

GS: Where did he take you?

AA: We went to the hospital in Manbij, the headquarters of what was known as the Daesh 'department for terror attacks and external operations'. The scene was apocalyptic: there were wounded Frenchmen, lying there groaning with their legs blown off. Even on the verge of death, some of them still clutched their weapons. One of them was still wearing an explosive belt with wires dangling off it. Some were handcuffed to their beds: Syrian army prisoners or Kurds. The doctor in charge of the hospital made no distinction: a wounded man is a wounded man. We spent four days there, basically so that Samy's leg could get better. The only activity consisted of going to pray five times per day in an improvised prayer room. Samy was resting and didn't talk much. On the second day, one of his friends, a Moroccan, was jumping up and down with joy. I found this a bit strange, given the general atmosphere of the place. In fact, it was 28 June 2014, the eve of a very significant event.

GS: The proclamation of the Islamic State on 29 June by al-Baghdadi, who declared himself the caliph? From that moment on, Daesh started to become a radically new type of organisation compared to other jihadist groups.

AA: Yes, and that's when I gave Mouna's letter to Samy, hoping that this would change the situation. He went away to read the letter alone and we didn't speak about it again. There was a heavy atmosphere between us.

Then we drove down to the other end of the town and bedded down in what had been a police station. That night, I slept outside on the terrace beneath the stars, it was very hot and I needed to breathe a bit. I felt stifled. We got up at three in the morning to eat and pray, before going back to bed again.

That morning, the caliphate was proclaimed. At about 8.00am, I heard shots going off all around the town and, at first, I thought an attack was under way. Samy didn't seem to care one way or the other, he just stared into the distance, with his gun over his shoulder. He really had the look of a loyal soldier, confident but rather jaded. The men were all congratulating each other and Samy eventually joined in, a vague smile crossing his lips. I think that we only exchanged words a couple of times in four days. While he used to talk a lot with his mother and his sisters, with me he just clammed up.

Later on, we went to an internet café and I noticed that he never missed an opportunity to apply the precepts of Daesh. He upbraided the owner who had dared to have some music playing. I saw the look of contempt in the eyes of this old man who eventually turned off the radio, giving in to what he must have considered to be a ridiculous whim on the part of this ignorant young man.

I had the feeling that I was getting nowhere, that it was impossible to really talk with Samy, and that the whole thing seemed to be a waste of time. I no longer had the energy to try to change his mind.

GS: So you turned back so soon? You felt that you wouldn't be able to make Samy come home?

AA: I think that I needed to go to Syria in order to realise this. There was no going back as far as he was concerned; nor, sadly, had there been any improvement in our relationship. In Syria, I lost my son a second time.

GS: How did you get back? Saying goodbye must have been heart-rending.

AA: A car was leaving for the Turkish border the following morning at 9.00am. We kissed each other. I would have gladly taken a photo, but I didn't want to make him feel awkward. Once I was in the car, we gave each other a quick wave, and after that I didn't look back. I thought that this might be the last time I saw him. It was windy and dusty, and there were graves by the roadside. As the kilometres went by, I thought of the poem Victor Hugo wrote for his drowned daughter, Léopoldine: 'Tomorrow, at dawn, at that hour when the land lies bleached, I will set out . . .' ('*Demain, dès l'aube, à l'heure où blanchit la campagne, je partirai . . .*')

Terrible thoughts went through my head: if something

happened to him, where could I mourn his grave? How could I come back here with my wife and daughters? How could I grieve if he died here and we never found his body? It was 1 July 2014.

As soon as I got back to the hotel in Gaziantep, I booked a return plane ticket to Charleroi leaving two days later via Istanbul. I was expecting to be stopped by the police for going to Syria, but nothing of the sort happened.

I feared the worst for my son, and I was powerless.

2

Life Before

AA: Georges, I can imagine how difficult this must be for you, but can you tell me what happened on 13 November 2015, after you saw Lola at the swimming pool?

GS: Actually, it was quite an ordinary day for me. It would make more sense to talk about 14 November 2015, as it was only after midnight that everything stopped being ordinary ... On the evening of the 13th, when the drama was unfolding, I didn't watch television or look at my computer. I didn't watch the France–Germany match; I'm one of those Frenchmen who, although not totally immune to the joys of the beautiful game, only really take an interest in football every four years, when the World Cup comes around. I probably spent the last part of the evening reading, as usual, and my wife and I went to bed without any idea what was happening in Paris and at the stadium in Saint-Denis.

At about 1.00am, we were woken up by the telephone ringing. It was my son, Clément, and he had never called us so late at night before. My wife Emmanuelle answered and, as I could hear that the call was going on and on, I also got up. She put the phone down, took my hands in hers and summed up the conversation: terror attacks in Paris, many deaths at the Bataclan, Lola was there, no reply from her mobile.

Lola

AA: Can you tell me about Lola? Where was she born? What was she like?

GS: Lola was born in Tarbes, in the Hautes-Pyrénées region of southwest France. We already had two boys and wanted a girl. For the first two, we hadn't wanted to know their sex before they were born; for the third, we were too impatient not to ask. After a close call when we thought we were going to lose the baby, the pregnancy went well and Lola came into the world on 6 December 1986. The labour was very quick: she was born before the gynaecologist could get there and the midwife only just had time to put her gloves on!

Lola was always delightful: as a baby, as a child, as a teenager and as a young woman. What really stood out about her, and is still true after her death, was her ability to form deep and above all long-lasting friendships with people possessed of extraordinary human qualities. She was an extrovert and always attentive to the needs of others, including strangers; in the winter, she wouldn't hesitate to call the social services hotline if she saw someone sleeping in the street. She was very attuned to the needs of others, and their suffering.

She was also always amazingly dynamic. When she was growing up, she took part in loads of sports and cultural activities, it was all part of her adventurous side. She enjoyed taking risks and was a constant whirl of activity, until she would drop from exhaustion. Whether it was on the crazy rides at Disneyland, galloping on a horse in Egypt, or on her roller-skates in Paris, she always went charging forwards, devouring life as if she knew that it wouldn't last.

AA: The way that you describe Lola, she seemed to have an almost sun-like quality.

GS: It's true, many wonderful people seemed to gravitate around her. She was like a magnet, full of joy. We always had the impression that she felt good about herself, even in difficult times such as during adolescence. This is how we can help others: one needs to love oneself before one can love others.

AA: How were things between your children? Things can get complicated when three people are involved.

GS: Our three children all have very different personalities, and this is itself a source of richness. Clément, the eldest, is very assertive and rational. He's a big chap and is probably the one who looks most like me. When he was little, he used to have a temper, but he also had a great sense of humour. Today, he's a lawyer, but he's also got an artistic streak, which made him think about working in the film industry, especially when he was having a hard time in the early years of his law studies. He wasn't putting much work in and was spending too much time mucking around, but the day he discovered moot competitions, it all came together: he could mix acting with the law! Being a natural orator, he had everything it takes to succeed. Now he's a specialist in employment law, which I'm not unhappy about. He always did have a social conscience.

My second son, Guilhem, is a different kettle of fish. He's a dreamer who developed a passion for drawing from an early age. A real non-conformist, he's always followed his own path. For example, spelling was absolute purgatory for him for a long time, because he couldn't see why he should obey a set of rules when writing, but once he saw the point of it, he never made a single mistake again. When we went skiing and he took lessons, the whole group would turn left, and ... he would turn right. I think he ended up being the eccentric in the family, the rebel. Today, he draws, using images to tell stories which take place in a fantasy universe. This is all the more important as it became a refuge for him after losing his sister in 2015.

The three of them were very close-knit. This is exactly what we wanted when we decided to have the children close together. Even though having three of them, as you suggest, meant that it was often us two against three! When they were children, Guilhem would swing from one side to the other, as the mood took him. Clément would be playing video games while the others watched him. He was the leader, and he was the one who set the agenda, so to speak. When the three of them were together, we would listen to them,

Emmanuelle and I, without always understanding what they were talking about …

We were happy to find out about things thanks to them and to see how they complemented and loved each other. Lola made us all laugh, not only with her jokes, but also because she had a very sonorous laugh, which was uniquely recognisable.

The South

AA: You said that Lola was born in the Hautes-Pyrénées. Are you from the region?

GS: My wife Emmanuelle and I first met when we were living in Béziers, in the Hérault region of southern France, but it was in Montpellier, where we were both studying medicine in the mid-1970s, that we fell in love and began living together. We've been together for more than forty years now, which isn't so common these days! And it was actually thanks to my wife, and quite early in our life together, that I first visited the Arab world. Emmanuelle's parents were teachers, and until 1966 they had worked on secondment to the school system of the newly independent Tunisia. They always told me that they had felt very awkward, as French expatriates, at receiving a much higher salary than their Tunisian colleagues. At the start of our relationship, Emmanuelle wanted to go back with me to the places she had known as a child. Habib Bourguiba's Tunisia was relatively free and open in comparison to other countries on the shores of the Mediterranean, where kings, dictators and military regimes held sway. But this openness was only relative: we had to pretend that we were married in order to share a room, and our hosts had to pretend to believe us. In any case, I don't think I considered these political questions too deeply at the time, but I did discover a universe which has never ceased to fascinate me since.

On the professional side of things, after gaining some experience of psychiatry, emergency medicine, gynaecology and obstetrics and gastro-enterology, in my sixth year I embarked on an internship which would seal my future career. It was 1981 and the head of the department, Professor André Mandin, was a remarkable character: he was a charismatic man, highly cultured, a great clinician, teacher and humanist ... but also autocratic and difficult to work with. My placement with his department was only meant to last four months, but I ended up working as an intern there for two years. I certainly showed tenacity, as it wasn't always easy! This slightly crazy professor steered me towards the public health area and encouraged me to write a thesis on the frequency and causes of handicaps in elderly people.

In 1982, Jack Ralite, the minister of health under François Mitterrand, had the bright idea of creating regional health observatories (ORS, *Observatoires régionaux de santé*) whose job it would be to identify the major health problems in the various regions of France. The ORS in Languedoc-Rousillon, a region in the south of France with an ageing population, had launched a study into the health of elderly people, and this corresponded exactly to the subject of my thesis. So, I was duly taken on as a researcher. At the same time as carrying out this study, I also got my specialist public health qualifications.

AA: That's quite an achievement! How did you end up living in Tarbes?

GS: Clément, our first child, was born in July 1982, while I was working on my thesis. His arrival meant I had to take some decisions about my career, as my wife was still a student. I couldn't work in a hospital, as I hadn't taken my intern exam. My job at the ORS wasn't secure. So, my public health professor, René Baylet, advised me to take the national exam to become a public health physician, which I passed at the end of 1983. This meant that I became a state employee, which is not the most lucrative way to practise medicine, but it did offer the advantage of ensuring financial stability for my family. This was all the more pressing seeing as my wife was expecting Guilhem, our second son.

That said, the path that I had chosen did bring with it a certain number of constraints, particularly in geographical terms. First there was a year's training at the National School of Public Health in Rennes, Brittany, before I could select a post. And between the end of this training year in 1984 and my first posting, I had to do one year's national service, during which I worked in the emergency and intensive care unit of the university hospital in Sète, on the southwestern coast. It was in 1986 that I could at last begin my first job as a public health physician in Tarbes.

Between Algeria and France

GS: And you, Azdyne, tell me about your family, I'm curious to know more about your wife and children.

AA: I met Mouna in 1979 on a flight from Annaba to Paris. She was in the seat next to me. She was beautiful and reading the Koran in French. I don't know whether this was out of religious conviction or simply fear of being on a plane. I kept a discreet eye on her throughout the flight and we only spoke to each other once we had landed in Paris. She was on her way back to her family in Nancy, in eastern France, and I plucked up the courage to offer to accompany her to the Gare de l'Est in Paris. At the time, I was working in the film industry in Paris, I was chasing after impossible dreams, and chasing a lot of girls, and I'd never told a woman I loved her. Was she going to be the one? After kissing her goodbye on the station platform, I confided to a friend: 'She's going to be my wife!' Bursting out with laughter, he replied: 'Azdyne, you're an incorrigible skirt-chaser ... You've only known her for fifteen minutes; in half an hour you'll have forgotten her!'

GS: Was it long before you heard from her again?

AA: When she got back home, she sent me a card to thank me. When I returned from San Francisco, where I'd been on holiday after working on a film, I found her card, but didn't dare get in touch with her. Then she sent me a letter, and that was when we agreed to meet up. I went to visit her in Lorraine, where she was living with her family, and we began seeing each other. The fourteen-year age gap between us didn't bother us. She was working as a doctor's secretary and, as for me, I was earning a good living in the film industry. I was living in the exclusive 16th *arrondissement* and driving around in a sports car. I would go and see her regularly and we got married a year later, in 1981.

GS: Was it long before your children came along?

AA: Alya was born three years later, in 1984, in Paris. We were living in a little bedsit that I was renting in the 16th *arrondissement* and when Samy arrived in 1987, we moved to the cheaper 15th *arrondissement*. When our youngest daughter, Maïssa, was born in 1993, we needed more space. I didn't have the money to stay in central Paris, so we moved out of the city itself, to Drancy in Seine-Saint-Denis, where we still live today.

GS: Where is Mouna from? Was she born in France?

AA: Her parents were Algerian but she was born and brought up in France; so she had a traditional side and a modern side at the same time. I wasn't often at home; I was moving around a lot. My job meant that I had to do a lot of travelling and I know that this wasn't easy for her, especially once the children came along.

An absent father

GS: When trouble comes along, are you someone who likes to slug it out, or do you prefer to make a run for it?

AA: For me, life is synonymous with movement. I worked in a four-star hotel in Paris, near the Champs-Élysées, before picking up a few jobs in the neighbourhood and finally winding up by accident in the film industry. It was all thanks to a friend of mine, Muriel, who worked in a temping agency. I just had time to do an accelerated training course, and Muriel got me straight into a contract with a film production company, Technisonor, which in those days was the equivalent of Radio Monte Carlo for television.[10] The company offices were on the rue Magellan, between avenue Marceau and the most beautiful avenue in the world, the Champs Élysées. It really was a different planet.

GS: So you found yourself plunged into the world of cinema almost by accident?

AA: Yes, I was working the switchboard, acting as an interface between the various teams: the producers, the actors, the technicians, etc. I found myself working on a film by the legendary New Wave director Claude Chabrol, who put me at my ease the moment we met. I said to him: 'I'm very pleased to meet you, Monsieur Chabrol.' And he said: 'Call me Claude, my lad! It'll be easier.' I felt proud and delighted.

Very quickly, I rose to be assistant editor on the serial *Les Chevaux du soleil* by Jules Roy, set in colonial Algeria, before working as a production manager and then getting behind

---

10 Translator's note: French television consisted only of state-run channels until 1982 (commercial radio stations had been legalised in 1981),
so independent production companies were somewhat comparable to
broadcasters operating from outside French territory, such as Radio
Monte Carlo in Monaco.

the camera as an assistant cameraman. I even had some small acting roles! I was proud that I had come from nowhere, with no connections whatsoever, yet had managed to break into this world. At last I was getting my own back after years spent doing odd jobs here and there, and I was driving around in a Simca Bagheera sports car. I even set up my own production company, 'Ciné film production'. I was leaving behind the lethargy of my youth and watching hundreds of films a year. It really was a frenetic period.

GS: So Samy didn't see much of you? Were you an absent father?

AA: Yes, you're probably right. I needed to keep moving; it was a question of survival for me. My wife never really stopped me either and, with hindsight, I sometimes wish she had. Maybe a firmer hand would have calmed me down and meant that I was around a bit more for everyone, above all for Samy.

GS: What you describe reminds me of the great explorer Théodore Monod. His family admired him enormously yet, while he loved his father, his son resented the fact that he had so often been away from them. Because what Monod loved more than anything else was being out in the desert.

Today, when I think of all the attention I lavish on my granddaughter, I get the feeling that I was sometimes kept apart from my own children by my work. They've never complained about it, but it's true that our life as a family was to a large extent dictated by the postings that I chose to further my career. I think that on the whole I was present

57

as a father, I was there in the evenings and at the weekend, and if I'd had the opportunity to fly off to the other side of the world, I wouldn't have gone without my family. There were times when I'd be away from the children for a few days because of work – and I did once go on a sailing trip – but I could never have been away from them for weeks at a time. I already felt guilty that my wife had had to put her own career on hold in order to follow me and look after the kids . . . In that respect, I'm far from being perfect either.

AA: It's hard being a parent. There's no instruction manual and you don't always get it right. I sometimes feel guilty as well, telling myself that I should have spent more time at home, but at the same time, I was trying to do my best for them. Did they miss me? Yes, maybe. Did Samy turn bad because of me? Nobody will ever know. The hard times that I had experienced when I was young shaped my future life: I was frustrated and I wanted to get away.

GS: I'm not sure it's possible to establish a link between your absence and the path taken by Samy, as radicalisation is a complex phenomenon. Had he mentioned that he missed you being there?

AA: I did talk about this with my wife recently, which is something we hadn't done for a long time. Samy clearly was affected by it, and he often said so to his mother. I definitely didn't give enough thought to my parental shortcomings, which led to his feelings of humiliation later on.

Living abroad

AA: And what about you, Georges, you said that you had various postings. Where did you live?

GS: The children spent their early years in Tarbes. Every weekend we took them to the mountains. The Pyrenees are a paradise for nature-lovers. In the summer we went hiking; in the winter we skied. We lived in a house with a garden ... it was lovely! Workwise, it wasn't so idyllic. In order to come with me, my wife Emmanuelle took a job as a doctor in a centre treating alcoholics, where she wasn't very happy. As for me, I was enjoying my work, but I had itchy feet. So we left the Pyrenees in June 1991 and went to live in Martinique, where I had managed to get a transfer to the Regional Health Inspectorate for Guyana and the French Antilles. Over there my work essentially involved organising healthcare services on the island, while Emmanuelle took up a post as a school doctor and also worked as a locum.

It was a real family adventure, and for two and a half years we travelled all over the place. We didn't live in the capital, Fort-de-France, but in a local village, or 'commune' called Ducos. We were still close to nature, although it was different to what we had known before, consisting of the sea, beaches, coral reefs, and also tropical forests and volcanoes. Some Martiniquan friends who were keen sailors took us around the island on their boat to Sainte-Lucie, and Lola loved this trip. She also played a lot of video games with her brothers and liked doing 'boys' stuff'. She was always laughing; she loved what we were doing and she never complained about anything.

AA: What was it like 'integrating' into Martiniquan society? Did you feel what we, as immigrants in France, have all felt at one time or another?

GS: We did make friends with Martiniquans, but it's true that you're easily pigeonholed on the basis of the colour of your skin. For the children, it was a big culture shock, and school acted as a stabilising influence for them. Lola began primary school when we got there and I think that the children got a great deal out of the experience, although it was tougher for the boys as relations between the pupils – and even with the teachers – could sometimes be violent. They did have a number of good friends in the neighbourhood, though. Lola never had any problems, as far as I could tell. She was too young to understand much, and she always had an amazing ability to make friends.

As for me, things were not always made easy by the fact that I was perceived within my profession as a representative of the French state, which was considered distant, centralising and condescending, and by some even colonialist and racist. Emmanuelle probably witnessed more of the social problems in Martinique, both in her work as a school doctor, where she occasionally saw children who were the victims of domestic violence, and when she worked as a locum and had to go at night into areas on the edges of the shantytowns.

AA: Did you return to France after your time in Martinique?

GS: No, from 1993 to 1998 we went to live in Egypt, and the five years we spent there were just as surprising, although the surroundings were very different. I had made some contacts with the French Mission for International Cooperation, which was based in Sainte-Lucie. My job in Martinique had mainly involved organising treatment, whereas my real interests lay in preventive healthcare. I therefore felt like a change, and one day a colleague from the Ministry of Foreign Affairs called me to ask if I would be willing to oversee Franco-Egyptian medical cooperation in Cairo. I said yes straight away (with the agreement of my wife, of course!). I'm not as spontaneous and impulsive as you are, but some words of wisdom – taken from Hippocrates' aphorisms – which I inherited from my mentor, the professor of medicine André Mandin, tell us that 'opportunity is fleeting'. So you have to grasp it when it appears.

Egypt had always loomed large in my imagination, my fascination having begun with my history lessons at secondary school, the sword and sandal epics of Cecil B. DeMille, Lawrence of Arabia, not forgetting Asterix and Cleopatra of course! As for Emmanuelle, even if she was a bit concerned by the spate of terror attacks that had recently happened in Egypt, she was tempted by the idea of living in an Arab country and encouraged me to go.

AA: I remember that period and the attack on the Semiramis Hotel in Cairo in 1993.

GS: Yes, on 26 October 1993, a French law professor, Fernand Boulan, and two of his American colleagues were gunned down with automatic weapons in this major hotel, right in the centre of Cairo. At the time the Egyptian authorities tried to play down the affair so as not to scare off tourists, and claimed that it was an isolated act, carried out by a mentally ill individual. Four years later, however, the same man, along with his brother, would go on to carry out a second attack which killed nine German tourists and their Egyptian driver on Tahrir Square, right in front of the Museum of Cairo. The two brothers were sentenced to death and welcomed the judgement with cries of 'Allahu Akbar!'

So, when we arrived in November 1993, the Semiramis Hotel attack had just happened. We had left our quiet little corner of the tropics to immerse ourselves in Egypt, where Islamist terrorism was beginning to strike.

AA: I don't know what to say; it's terrible ...

GS: Absolutely, especially when you know how the story ends twenty years later. At the beginning, we felt a bit worried, especially Emmanuelle, but we got used to it. The years following our arrival were pretty quiet, with no attacks on tourists at any rate. During this period, however, France suffered a wave of attacks carried out by the Armed Islamic Group of Algeria (GIA), which culminated in July 1995 with the bombing of the Saint-Michel underground station in central Paris. The gas bottle packed with metal bolts which exploded that day killed eight people and wounded more than one hundred. We said to ourselves that, at the end of the day, we weren't taking much more of a risk living in Cairo than if we'd been in Paris ...

AA: Were you able to see much of Egypt despite this? I know the country well, having lived there myself.

GS: Oh yes, from the north to the south and the east to the west! The only area which had the reputation of being dangerous was Middle Egypt, between the south of Cairo and the north of Luxor. We were advised against taking the train to Luxor, so we went there by plane, as we did for Aswan. We also took a river cruise between these two magical cities, and another one on Lake Nasser, created by the high dam, up to the temple of Abu Simbel. We toured the rest of the country by car, sometimes driving hundreds of kilometres through the desert to get to Sinai – which at that time wasn't the Islamist stronghold it has since become – and the western oases of Bahariya, Farafra and Kharga, the White Desert, Alexandria, El Alamein with its deeply moving military cemetery, Marsa Matruh, where Rommel set up his headquarters in 1942, and Siwa Oasis, just next to the Libyan border. Maybe you know all these places yourself?

AA: Siwa? That's the oasis where a lot of Berber people live, isn't it?

GS: That's right! Siwi is a Berber dialect. One of our English archaeologist friends spoke it, and his wife gave Lola English lessons. Siwa is also the only place in Egypt where they eat couscous. It's one of the most beautiful spots on Earth, a vast palm grove on the edge of the Grand Erg, the sandy desert with immense dunes. There are dozens of natural springs creating pools of bubbling water which you can swim in. In the middle is a ruined fortress which crumbles a bit more every time it rains, as it's made of dried mud. Mind you, on average it only rains once every thirty years! In the past, the inhabitants used to rebuild it after each rain; now, they've moved into little shacks made of brick and concrete, which are less picturesque, but probably easier to live in.

AA: You did see the pyramids, though, didn't you?

GS: Yes, and not just the three big pyramids beside the Sphinx on the Giza plateau, but also all the other ones which line the western bank of the Nile – the bank of the dead – between Meidum and Abu Rawash, passing through the amazing site of Saqqara, which the Egyptologist Jean-Philippe Lauer spent his life exploring and reconstructing, stone by stone. We were even lucky enough to have a tour of Saqqara in his company, before his death in 2001, at the age of ninety-nine. I have to say that the children actually found riding horses around the pyramids rather more interesting than listening to Egyptologists telling stories! Lola was particularly taken by these rides, and she was always ready to take off at a fast gallop! She was pretty good at taming Arab thoroughbreds, which are quite small but difficult to handle. I must say that galloping across the Giza plateau in the shadow of the pyramids was an amazing experience!

But I think that the thing we liked the most in Egypt was the street life, the old town of Cairo with its shabby mosques, its brightly coloured, beaten-up shopfronts, its smells and its people who always manage to laugh and dance in spite of their poverty. Life was everywhere in Egypt: something was always happening in the street or elsewhere. I know that a lot of people are put off by the chaos, the noise and the dust, but we were like children, marvelling at everything we saw. The memories are etched on our minds for ever.

AA: Did you take the opportunity to learn Arabic? It's the ideal country for that.

GS: Emmanuelle learnt Arabic to a better standard than me. The people I was dealing with in my work spoke English or French. But I really like the Arabic spoken in Cairo; it's a lively form of the language, full of images. Unfortunately, the children didn't learn it at school, as the French *lycée* (high school) in Cairo wasn't very open to the teaching of Arabic, which is a shame. They did get a very good grounding in English, though, as we were very much part of the expat community, and they had lots of English-speaking friends.

AA: Like you, I love Egyptian street life; each day is a piece of unending theatre. Professionally speaking, did you gain much from your stay?

GS: The experience was in equal parts inspiring and disappointing. I was setting up collaborative projects between French and Egyptian institutions with the aim of improving the Egyptian health system, but also with a view to reinforcing the links between our two countries and helping maintain the presence and influence of the French language. I wanted to do something useful, and I had the impression that I was succeeding. I worked with the French ambulance and emergency service (SAMU) and the Egyptian Health Ministry on a project to improve how emergency cases were dealt with, and I helped *Médecins sans frontières* set up an operation in Egypt to help child labourers and street children in Cairo. But although all the projects we worked on were very worthwhile, none of them really came to anything because of corruption, inertia and the vagaries of politics. I don't imagine things have changed much since, as Egypt still has the reputation of being a bureaucratic pyramid ... That's what I regret the most; at the same time, I learned a lot about international cooperation and developmental aid.

AA: How did the kids get on over there? Was it more difficult to fit in than in Martinique?

GS: The children went to school at the French *lycée* in Cairo, which at that time was situated in Maadi, a leafy suburban district with attractive houses. So that's where we decided to live. We had a comfortable apartment, with a '*baouab*', or porter, who like most of his colleagues was from Nubia, standing guard at the gate. By the standards of Cairo, it was an affluent neighbourhood, with a very cosmopolitan population. We had French, American and English friends, as well as a political exile from Syria. At most, only half the students at the *lycée* were actually French; there were various other nationalities there, including many Egyptians. My son Clément had a Palestinian friend, whose father had been one of Yasser Arafat's bodyguards.

AA: Well fancy that, I know Maadi too! It was originally built as a new town by an English firm to very exacting standards. It's one of the few developments in Cairo and its suburbs, and today maybe even the only one, to have been laid out according to a proper plan, following a grid pattern. There are lots of trees as well, which is unfortunately unusual in Cairo.

GS: Yes, a nice peaceful neighbourhood ... where Ayman al-Zawahiri, the leader of Al-Qaeda, was born! He started out as a doctor, like his parents. Hosni Mubarak was also held in Maadi prison after the revolution in 2011.

AA: What are your favourite memories of Lola from when you lived there?

GS: As always, she managed to make friends in Maadi and she was very happy in the neighbourhood and at school. She really loved to ride horses, beside the pyramids or at the Maadi Sporting Club, where she took riding lessons – it didn't matter where. She also loved being outdoors: on the long drives into the desert with Bedouin guides where we'd pitch our tent in an oasis or beneath a sand dune; our weekend trips to the Wadi Degla valley, where one day we almost stepped on a horned viper; the Red Sea, the corals, going snorkelling to look at tropical fish ... We used to go to Sharm El Sheikh and Ras Muhammad on the tip of the Sinai, but we also visited the coast along the Gulf of Aqaba, up to Eilat in Israel, which we crossed into on foot through the border post at Taba. We also went to Jordan, where we saw Petra, Jerash, the Crusader fortress of Kerak and Mount Nebo, from where we could see the Dead Sea and the Promised Land, just like Moses. What Lola enjoyed the most about all this was meeting people. She retained

GEORGES SALINES & AZDYNE AMIMOUR

this taste for travel as an adult, exploring Korea, the United States, Cyprus and Israel, and always keeping things basic, staying with local people. I was impressed by this, as when I travel, I prefer things to be planned in advance and a bit more comfortable.

AA: Did you leave Egypt because of the new series of terror attacks?

GS: No, we left because of work. Emmanuelle was working as a doctor at the French *lycée*, but she wanted to develop her career after having put it on hold to follow me around the world and have some spare time to spend with the children. While in Egypt, she'd done a public health course and passed the national exam to be a public health physician. So she'd ended up following the same path as I had, only a few years later, and we went back to France so that she could do her training year at the *École des hautes études en santé publique* in Rennes.

That said, terrorism did leave its mark on our last year in Egypt. The Deir el-Bahari attack on 17 November 1997, at the temple of Hatshepsut in Luxor, shocked us deeply. That day, a group of Islamist gunmen killed more than sixty tourists, including thirty-six people from Switzerland. These helpless innocents were caught in a trap, with no way of getting out given the layout of the place: a series of terraces under the blazing sun, offering absolutely no cover from the terrorists shooting from above. Out of all the attacks that I would hear about up until the killings in Paris in January 2015, this was the one which affected

68

me the most, as my colleagues from the embassy who had gone to visit the survivors in various hospitals brought back harrowing tales.[11] We later learned that the terrorists were all medical students. How could future doctors commit such an act? How could that beacon of Arab civilisation that Egypt had once been now become the theatre of such barbarism? The full story of this attack has never been told, as the terrorists all died in somewhat unclear circumstances during their escape. It's difficult to say whether they were killed by the police or committed suicide. Tracts belonging to Al-Gama'a al-Islamiyya ('the Islamic Group') were found with their bodies, but the investigation was closed in 2000.

AA: When you came back to France, did your children become the objects of great curiosity at school?

GS: Funnily enough, when we came back to Paris, the other kids at school weren't all that interested by their life in Egypt. They were above all made to feel that they came from somewhere very different, and they weren't familiar with all the little codes you need to know at school in Paris. For instance, they couldn't speak Parisian 'verlan' back slang![12]

---

11 Translator's note: a reference to the attack on the offices of the satirical magazine *Charlie Hebdo* and the linked hostage-taking and killings at a kosher supermarket in Paris on 7 and 9 January 2015 respectively.

12 Translator's note: '*verlan*' is a form of slang that originated in Paris and involves inverting the syllables of a word or phrase. For instance, the noun '*femme*' (woman) is split into two syllables, pronounced 'fa' and 'meuh', which are then recombined in reverse order to produce the *verlan* expression: '*meuf*'.

For Lola, who was only twelve, the transition was easier than for the boys. Growing up isn't always easy . . .

So, now tell me about Samy. Was he a happy child?

From the 16th *arrondissement* to Drancy

AA: Mouna and I were over the moon to have Samy, as he was a boy, the first-born. In Muslim families, that's always a source of great joy. I know that for you, it was the other way round, because when Lola came along, she was your first daughter.

GS: And our last . . .

AA: Of course.

GS: How did Samy's arrival change your lives?

AA: After his arrival, we moved from the 16th to the less upmarket 15th *arrondissement*. The apartment was bigger, but I had to do some work fixing it up. There was a shop space on the ground floor, where I opened a clothing store, and later a dairy shop. The thing I remember the most clearly from these first years was Samy's circumcision. He was two and a half and we took him to the hospital to have it done. I think having the operation was very traumatic for him; he was screaming at us to stop in his toddler-speak. I explained to him that, in our religion, circumcision was a sign of our bond with God. When Samy was three, in 1989, we moved to Drancy in Seine-Saint-Denis, just outside Paris. I was delighted with the pleasant, spacious apartment that we found there. The local council was run by the Communists under Jean-Claude Gayssot, who, in 1997, would become a government minister in Lionel Jospin's administration.

GS: You went from the 16th to the 15th *arrondissement*, then the '93'?[13] That must have been quite a shock ...

AA: If I'm honest with you, Georges, I can't say that the people were all that nice in the 16th, and in Drancy I was able to reconnect with my Algerian roots. I made friends with people I could trust and Samy would go to judo classes with their children. As he was rather withdrawn, judo was a way for him to let off steam. At home, he didn't talk much; when he was playing sports, he loosened up. He liked the team aspect of football and he made a lot of friends that he kept into adulthood, even up until ... he went out to Syria. At the time, I wanted him to become a footballer.

GS: You're kidding!

AA: That's not all: after that I wanted him to be an airline pilot! I taught him all the aeronautical terms – 'alpha, bravo, charlie' ... I also taught him all the world's capital cities, which he thought was great fun. I didn't manage to get him interested in music, though. Maybe because of my restless

---

13 Translator's note: mainland France is divided into 96 administrative areas, called *départements* (departments), which are, with some exceptions, numbered alphabetically. '93' refers to the department of Seine-Saint-Denis, immediately to the northwest of Paris proper. Although the district of Drancy is only five miles from central Paris, it is not considered as being part of the capital, but rather as belonging to the *banlieue*, the suburbs around Paris dominated by high-rise housing estates with a reputation for crime and poverty, and populated by a high proportion of minority ethnic residents, including many Muslims.

nature, I wanted him to discover all sorts of different things. At primary school he was a good child, well behaved, and never caused any trouble.

GS: You wanted him to be a footballer, a pilot . . . Perhaps these were your own dreams rather than his? Later on, did he want to carry on the things you had introduced him to?

AA: That was my aim at the beginning; I wanted him to be curious, with a thirst for knowledge, but children move from one thing to another . . .

GS: Like you!

AA: Maybe I never really grew up, and never wanted to become a proper adult . . . It's possible. In any case, by trying to get my children interested in various things, I wanted to avoid them having to go through the same things that I had known: ignorance, poverty, other problems. I had got away from all that and I wanted to give them every possible advantage.

Islam

GS: Did you teach them about your religion?

AA: I tried to pass on French and Algerian, as opposed to 'Muslim', values. My wife and daughters never covered their hair; my attitude was that we were in France and we should adapt to the country in which we were living. But, as I was telling you, Mouna has kept in touch with her traditional side, in a positive way; she would sometimes read the Koran in memory of her father, who first set her on the path of religion. A few times during Ramadan, we watched Mustapha Akkad's film *The Message*, with Anthony Quinn. I explained to Samy that there were actually one hundred and twenty-four thousand prophets: Jesus, Moses, and many others, but I could clearly see that he wasn't all that interested. Where we lived, you didn't see any veiled women or particularly religious families, and perhaps that's what troubled him later on. As for his friends, they came from a variety of backgrounds.

GS: Do you think that he experienced any discrimination at one time or another, either for being an Arab, or from his Muslim friends because of your rather minimalist approach to the practice of Islam?

AA: He got on well with all his classmates and never complained of being called a 'dirty Arab' or such like. And what if we'd stayed in Paris in the 16th *arrondissement*? That's a question that haunts me to this day. In Drancy, though, he was surrounded by diversity and tolerance, which is also a key characteristic of Islam. We lived in a four-storey block where from one landing to the next you could find families of every origin – Moroccan, Algerian, Tunisian, Romanian, French, Portuguese ... Richard, our neighbour from the same floor whom I've already told you about, a Sephardi Jew we got on really well with, played a big part in shielding us from prying eyes and the media after the 2015 attacks. We used to talk together late into the night. He was more chatty than me and taught me many things, like the fact that Joshua, the son of Nun, who was Moses' disciple, is supposed to be buried in

Ghazaouet, in Algeria. We also talked about Palestine and had the odd row when discussing the subject of Israel.

GS: Were you around during Samy's teenage years?

AA: It's true that I was often travelling. When I left the film industry, I went back to doing small-scale overseas trading, especially with Algeria, where I opened a sports equipment business. So, from when Samy was ten until he was eighteen, I spent a lot of time in Algeria, as well as in Pakistan and Indonesia where I had some items manufactured.

GS: A sports equipment business in Algeria? You don't pick the most straightforward ways to make a living!

AA: That's true, I sometimes ended up making two trips per week to Algiers. Mouna would stay at home and look after the children, so she followed Samy's development more closely. I went wherever I thought I could earn a crust, and I know that my son was proud of his father.

GS: I can see how a young teenager must have been in awe of a father like you, but where did Samy fit into all this? Did you have some fun times together?

AA: The best times that I spent with him were definitely during my 'Algerian period', from when he was seven, in 1994, to when he reached adulthood, around 2005. I was able to pay him some attention and still had some influence over him. We would share holidays in Algeria, the sea, a passion for football ... During the World Cup in 1998, I bought him a Brazil shirt and took him on a surprise visit to watch Ronaldo training. That was his dream. I also took him along to film sets in Paris, to women's football matches in Algeria where I had set up a team, and to boxing matches which I organised.

GS: Do you think today that the distance between you, because of all this travelling, was a problem for Samy? How were things with his sisters?

AA: The problem is that, even with the benefit of hindsight, he was always a mystery, including for Mouna, who saw him every day. Sometimes I had the feeling that there was a stranger in the house. He suffered from being stuck between his little sister, Maïssa, whom he hardly spoke with at all, and his big sister Alya. Once he'd gone to Syria, however, he relied on Maïssa for support, and she thought that they would become closer again. Alya was more able to get through to Samy, but she went away to live in Dubai. In any case, he would often shut himself away in his room when he was a teenager and didn't really talk with us. When Mouna heard him laugh, she felt reassured. She was quite protective of him, and when she was on the parent–teacher committee at his high school, she took his side when he was accused of having thrown a rubber at a school inspector. The accusation was false because a few days later another pupil confessed to the deed. I couldn't believe that Samy had done it, especially seeing as he would sometimes come back from school covered in bruises.

GS: Evidence of blows like that could suggest that, even if he wasn't the victim of discrimination, he might have had a hard time of it at school, as many adolescents do.

AA: Yes, he was a bit of a pushover, and easily led. His big sister Alya, on the other hand, was a tigress and often mocked him for being a 'little darling', probably our little darling – as his parents – because he was in the middle. As a teenager, he reminded me of many that you see today: withdrawn, taciturn, mysterious. After a lot of digging, I managed to get him to admit at eighteen that, 'Dad, I'm not happy.' I couldn't understand, as I thought that I'd given him all the things that I myself had never had.

GS: Perhaps you gave him what you yourself had lacked, but the recipe for happiness is complicated, especially when you're eighteen or twenty. You know how Paul Nizan's novel *Aden Arabie* begins: 'I was twenty. I'll never let anyone say that that's the best time of your life ...'

AA: Yes, that's probably true. What I can tell you, in any case, is that he spent a lot of time on the computer, and that's when he began watching those damned videos.

GS: Which videos?

AA: At one point, he was watching a lot of videos on the internet about 9/11 and Bin Laden. I would nose around and look over his shoulder. Once he yelled at me: 'Are you watching me? Do you think that if someone asked me to throw a grenade into a café, I'd do it?' I replied that, obviously, I trusted him completely not to do it. That was in 2006, and he was nineteen. I could tell that something wasn't right all the same; his class teacher had told us that he seemed distracted in the lead-up to his *baccalauréat* exams, but had a lot of ability. He advised us to go and see a psychologist, so we all went along with him once as a family, but there was no follow-up. A girl from his class would tell me later: 'Samy didn't talk much, but when he did say something, you could be sure it wouldn't be something stupid.'

9/11

GS: To my mind, 9/11 is an event which remains central to contemporary relations between the West and the Arab and Muslim world. There had already been numerous Islamist terror attacks in Iraq, Afghanistan, Somalia, Algeria, France, but not on American soil – with the exception of the 1993 attack on (let's not forget!) the World Trade Center. On 11 September 2001, the United States suffered a grievous blow with the collapse of the Twin Towers and the destruction of part of the Pentagon. The American reaction was massive and brutal with the war in Afghanistan and, above all, the invasion of Iraq, the latter justified on the basis of lies. Many Muslims who already took a dim view of the United States' unshakeable support for Israel came to the conclusion that the attacks had been the ideal pretext for a neo-colonial project. George W. Bush didn't help by calling for a 'crusade' against terrorism – all the more so given that the word 'crusade' translates literally as 'war of the cross' in Arabic. It was therefore inevitable that some people would imagine that the attacks had been organised with the aim of providing a pretext for this 'crusade'. The conspiracy theory had taken root and would spread throughout the entire world.

AA: Personally, I didn't always see the 'conspiracy' in the way you describe, but I did have an instinctive reaction, or a desire, to look for what might be hidden behind these events.

GS: What did you feel on 11 September 2001, when you saw the two towers of the World Trade Center collapse and the plane crash into one of the Pentagon buildings?

AA: Obviously, it was a big shock. I felt the same way as everyone else, that it was appalling. I was well aware that the United States had started many devastating wars in the name of freedom and their values, but why this attack? Samy was only fourteen at the time. He sat watching the images on the television while they talked about Al-Qaeda, Bin Laden. It seemed to be too much for him to take in. Later, I read theories which said that the attacks had been orchestrated, and I believed them, it's true, I admit it. In a way, it was a relief for me.

GS: If you're going to try spreading those half-baked ideas, it'll be hard for me to keep listening to you ...

AA: Like everyone, I was overwhelmed by that appalling spectacle. I saw the videos playing on a loop on TF1, but I found it all so unbelievable that I was sceptical about the whole thing.[14]

GS: But didn't you think about the victims? Didn't you see the videos of people throwing themselves from the top of the towers? It's terrible that you should think this was all a conspiracy, Azdyne.

---

14 Translator's note: TF1 is France's most-watched television channel.

AA: I didn't believe it was all a conspiracy, but I listened to different versions in order to draw my own conclusions. One is allowed to have doubts. I listened to specialists, experts, airline captains ... On the television, I saw the father of a victim holding up a placard with 'inside job' written on it. I wasn't the only one to have doubts.

GS: Conspiracy theories have existed for a very long time about all sorts of subjects. There'll always be someone presenting themselves as an expert and explaining how we never went to the Moon, how the CIA assassinated Kennedy or how the Earth is flat. It's all nonsense, but relatively harmless. By contrast, doubting what happened in New York and Washington on 11 September is a form of denial which is unbearably hurtful for the families of the victims. As you surely know, conspiracy theories quickly sprang up regarding 13 November 2015. Some people spread the idea that our intelligence services knew what was being planned and deliberately didn't intervene in time so that the authorities could subsequently impose a state of emergency. Others even claimed that the attacks hadn't happened at all, and that the victims in the photos were actors ... All that is not just untrue, but it also means more suffering for the families.

Azdyne, you know that there are also people who deny the Holocaust. Try to imagine a dialogue like ours between the son of a deportee liquidated in a concentration camp and the son of a brutal Nazi murderer. They're talking together when, all of a sudden, the victim's son realises that the man he's speaking to still believes that the death camps maybe never really existed . . . You can debate the existence of God without any major consequences, as nobody's sure about anything, but when it comes to 9/11, about which we know almost everything, it's impossible to have any doubts. In fact, I could lend you a special issue of a scientific journal devoted to these events, which also looks into the psychological mechanisms behind conspiracy theories. I hope that you'll be willing to read it.

AA: Yes, I will read it. I'd be very happy to be convinced, as a large part of what I've looked at so far on the subject of 9/11 has tended towards the sceptical view. I also found it hard to accept that the attack had been carried out by Muslims, indeed not just that attack but those which would follow as history went on. I feel no sympathy for Al-Qaeda and I'm not an Islamist, but I do retain a certain dislike for American policy in the Middle East and throughout the world.

GS: Me too, Azdyne, but there's no need to be a conspiracy theorist to see that! Do you think that the convictions which you had, and perhaps still have now, could have influenced Samy? Because conspiracy theories are a huge part of Daesh's ideological underpinnings.

AA: I know that Samy was very shy and easily led. I'm sure it would have been easy for him to get into conspiracy theories. I don't think he had the intellectual and emotional resources to resist manipulative people.

GS: Do you think that your absence during his formative years might have played a part in developing his convictions and causing his radicalisation?

AA: It's true that, during his adolescence, I would sometimes be away for several days a week, and sometimes for a whole month, like the time I was working in Senegal and Mali. After working in the film industry, I found it hard to get back into steady work, sitting behind a desk. Although Mouna would regularly complain about it, I thought that working abroad was the only way for me to earn some money and make a better life for us.

GS: But you had a home, a family and children who loved you. Have you ever had the feeling that you've been chasing after something your whole life?

AA: My children and my wife meant everything to me, but developing new projects was a way for me to keep moving up the social ladder; I didn't want to go back to doing menial jobs. There was nothing more for me in Paris . . . To tell the truth, it was quite unlike the normal path taken by immigrants: whereas they were coming to Europe to do low-skilled jobs, I was going abroad to earn my living and find a bit of excitement.

Islam and atheism

GS: So, as I understand it, the critical turning point in Samy's trajectory came when he was eighteen?

AA: Yes, I would say that, up until the *baccalauréat*, everything had been going fairly well. He had chosen the literature pathway, despite never reading anything, which was rather surprising. He had begun reading the Koran in

French, though, and I could see that he was starting to ask questions about Islam. Once he'd passed his exams, I therefore had the idea of sending him to Annaba, to the 'Cheikh Amimour El Hilali El Azhari' mosque, which had been built in honour of his grandfather. My father, you see, had been an advisor to the Ministry of Religious Affairs and, to pay tribute to him, the town authorities had turned an old church into a mosque. I learned from Samy's friends that he had begun praying and, from one day to the next, had started wearing a *qamis* to go to the mosque. I was concerned, but thought that this was probably better than drinking or taking drugs. So it was aged eighteen that he 'came back to religion' as they say, even if he was actually taking his first steps towards it.

GS: And at this time you and Mouna still weren't praying yourselves?

AA: No, not at this point. As a child, I'd been frustrated by the teaching methods and simplistic rules of Islam. As children, my brothers and sisters and I had had religion forced down our throats by my father, and I couldn't stand it anymore. For years, I rejected any sort of religious practice, and I wanted to leave my children to do what they wanted in that respect. I've only eaten pork once, because I didn't have any choice – but in such situations, it's authorised by the Koran. In the end, it was because of Samy that I started praying again, and Mouna began doing so regularly. I thought that 'accompanying' him in his faith was a way of protecting him. When I worked in the film industry, alcohol and drugs were everywhere. At home, with my wife, the mood was much calmer and more formal. Maybe Samy suffered from seeing me pulled between these two worlds?

GS: I do find your relationship with Islam a bit odd. You've rejected the traditional side of religion, which surely has something to do with the years you spent in Koranic school, but you don't question the fundamental bases of Islam, while not wanting to look into them more deeply either. You have your son circumcised and you don't eat pork, but you drink alcohol and don't say your prayers. You believe in God, but you might say that He remains rather distant for you. I'm an atheist, but when all's said and done, I get the impression that I take God much more seriously than you do!

AA: To tell the truth, my practice of Islam has always been quite free and has never been defined by strict principles. Could you tell me a bit about your atheism? In terms of spirituality, how did you and your wife raise your children?

GS: Emmanuelle and I brought up our children without hiding anything about what we thought ourselves, but without ever seeking to indoctrinate them either, whether in political or religious matters. If one of them had wished, for example, to practise Catholicism, we wouldn't have stood in their way, but none of the three turned out to be a believer. When I think back to your experiences, I suspect that the freedom of choice that we wanted to give them was probably subject to some unconscious limits. If they had wanted to believe in God, they wouldn't have had any precedent in our family to refer to, and religious yearnings probably involve a process of mimetism. As far as I'm concerned, my position is clear: belief without rational proof offends my scientific mind! And, since there is no proof, I don't have 'faith'. I sometimes even have trouble imagining what the God that religious people believe in is, exactly. Behind this word, they probably don't all see the same thing.

AA: God is a complex phenomenon which can't be reduced to simple terms.

GS: That's precisely my question: what is God? If He is considered to be the creator of the world, I would have trouble accepting this theory, as in my view it just boils down to replacing one mystery, that of the existence of the universe, with another, that of the existence of God – which is even more impenetrable. I find it simpler just to think that the world exists by itself.

If by 'God' you mean the thing which gives a moral sense to existence – the voice inside us which allows us to distinguish between good and evil – I also think that's a needlessly complicated way of looking at things. There are perfectly plausible explanations for the fact that man is an animal endowed with a sense of right and wrong which have no need of such metaphysical crutches: evolution may well have favoured the survival of those members of a tribe who were nicest to the others! Altruistic behaviour has also been observed among animals. Besides, our sense of morality has changed over time: religious commandments prescribe conduct seen as appropriate at the time, rather than an eternal divine truth. This is just as well, otherwise we'd still be burning witches and executing homosexuals ... The fundamentalists from all religions are the only ones who haven't grasped this.

As for the idea that God is the creator who, depending on our behaviour, rewards us in paradise or punishes us in hell after our death, that just seems absurd to me. I think the exact opposite of those believers who say: 'If there is nothing after death, then life has no meaning.' As far as I'm concerned, if there is an afterlife, if God knows in advance who will go to heaven or hell, if He is omniscient and 'everything is written', then why are we all sitting around in the waiting room?! That's why I'm an atheist.

AA: You could have been agnostic.

GS: That's true, but I define myself more as an atheist, and that doesn't mean that I am absolutely sure that God doesn't exist. I just apply the principle formulated by the fourteenth-century English philosopher William of Ockham known as 'Occam's razor': 'Entities should not be multiplied unnecessarily.' As the mathematician Bertrand Russell succinctly put it, I cannot prove that there is not a teapot orbiting the sun between the Earth and Mars, but as I have no reason to think that it does exist, it is reasonable to assume that it does not exist ... in the absence of proof to the contrary.

With God, it's the same thing: trying to put a sticking plaster over our ignorance by using the word 'God' is pointless. For a very long time, men were simply unable to imagine how the amazing diversity, complexity and (relative) perfection of animal and plant life on Earth could have arisen. They therefore assumed that it had been created by an intelligent being called 'God', until Darwin provided an incredibly simple model to explain everything, which explains not only why so many plants, animals and micro-organisms exist, but also why each of these creatures is complex and adapted for its own survival.

We haven't got so far in our understanding of the origin of the universe and the reality of what matter and energy really are. You can't start looking into modern physics without your head spinning. The more we move forward, the more particle physics essentially becomes a set of equations describing phenomena that our limited minds are incapable of visualising. We can't explain the mystery of the existence of the universe by assuming that it was created by God, because we don't know what God is, nor what created God. And if God wasn't created, then why does the universe need to have been?

AA: And what about the mystic poets, which we also have in Sufi Islam (Rumi, Ibn Arabi, Abd al Qadir al-Jilani, etc.), what do you think about them?

GS: I also have trouble understanding mysticism. I did get interested in the mystical experiences of the philosopher Simone Weil, who explained how Christ 'came down' and 'took' her, that in some way He came to find her. She considers in any case that man cannot go towards God alone, that he must first receive grace. Speaking for myself, nobody's ever come to get me! And if I suddenly began to feel a force, a higher presence, I would probably wonder whether I wasn't falling under the spell of a delusion. I can understand how Teresa of Ávila, who lived in the sixteenth century, might have taken her experiences of 'transverberation' with an angel – described by her in terms which today strike the reader for their obvious sexual dimension – at face value, but how could Simone Weil, who was a contemporary of Sigmund Freud, have been certain that her unconscious wasn't playing tricks on her?

AA: Can you say for sure that you know what your children believe today?

GS: I think I do, yes: they believe in themselves, for a start! Clément shares my vision of the world, but he doesn't like to proselytise. Rather than talk about philosophy or religion, he prefers to discuss politics with his friends (although they're probably more interested in video games and cinema to be honest). As for Guilhem, he enjoys intellectual debate and has practised the art of verbal jousting from a very young age. It's true that, when we lived in Martinique and Egypt, he was surrounded by children who were believers and were always trying to convert him. Today, he'll happily 'cross swords' on these topics on social media. My Lola didn't believe in God. At the top of her scale of values were friendship and respect for others. She was friends with a practising Jewish girl, Raphaëlle, who taught us a lot about Orthodox Judaism and Judaism in general. When she was eighteen, Lola went with her to Israel and discovered a world that she had no idea existed. Later, Raphaëlle made her *aliyah* to Tel Aviv, but she returned with a somewhat more nuanced perspective on her relation to Judaism.

AA: How can anyone be unmoved before the Holy Land and the three times holy city of Jerusalem?

GS: Unmoved, certainly not, but when she was over there, Lola wasn't touched by God's grace. She kept lasting memories of tourist sites, like the old town of Jerusalem, Tel Aviv and the Dead Sea, and she was deeply affected by her visit to the Yad Vashem memorial, devoted to the memory of the Holocaust. Like me, when I visited the centre, she was especially moved by the children's memorial, which is dug into the wall of a cave, with thousands of candles. However, she didn't come back with different views on the Israeli–Palestinian conflict; what interested her wasn't grand political systems and conflicts, but rather individuals. She was touched by people, whether they were Israelis, Palestinians, green, white or yellow, and that was one of her great qualities. Unlike me, she was never politically active, in the sense of being involved in party politics. I'm just thinking back to the way in which you tried to pass things on to Samy. When I was young, I was mixed up with every conceivable cause which sought to change the world. But Lola, well, she never campaigned for anything. We also learn things from our children.

Forging a political consciousness

AA: Did you campaign a lot when you were younger?

GS: Yes, my political awakening came very early on.

My interest in politics was first kindled by the discussions between my uncles and my father over Sunday lunch. To varying degrees, they were all on the left, but with enough shades of difference to cause arguments. I loved their often impassioned exchanges, even though I didn't understand everything they were saying. By contrast, I hated the racist diatribes that my paternal grandparents would sometimes launch into when I was there. While my uncles were left-wing intellectuals, my grandparents were from a much more working-class background. My grandfather voted 'Workers", but he was quite prejudiced, and I remember being shocked on various occasions, all the more so because I was very fond of him.[15]

AA: Your left-wing consciousness was already emerging. So, even when you were very young, did you position yourself against discrimination towards immigrants, for instance?

GS: Yes, particularly seeing as this was at the beginning of the 1970s and, as you've pointed out, right in the middle of the wave of immigration from Algeria. At that time, I wasn't yet ready to play an active part in politics, but I was gathering my ideas, reading the *Nouvel Observateur* and following debates on the television.[16] In my years at high school and

---

15 Translator's note: a reference to the SFIO (*Section française de l'internationale ouvrière*, French Section of the Workers' International), founded in 1905 and replaced in 1969 by the current Socialist Party.

16 Translator's note: *Le Nouvel Observateur* (rebranded *L'Obs* in 2014) is France's biggest political and cultural weekly. It has consistently maintained a left-leaning social-democratic stance.

lycée, I also began getting a sense of the wider world through cinema. I started going to a film club when I was thirteen or fourteen and I could sense my growing awareness during the discussions after the screenings. In particular, people would be talking about the Middle East and the Israeli-Palestinian issue, which was already a highly divisive subject. I would eagerly listen to these battles of oratory, and this was my first insight into what is dubbed the 'Orient'.

AA: Did you talk about France as well – about economics, social issues?

GS: Of course, as well as questions of societal attitudes, which really grabbed me, like the fight for abortion rights and the abolition of the death penalty. Very early on, I got interested in environmental issues. I even remember doing a presentation in class when I was around fifteen on a report produced by the Club of Rome in 1972 entitled 'The Limits of Growth'. Already at that time, people were telling us that we had exhausted the planet's resources and that it was time to take action . . . And that was forty-five years ago!

AA: I know, it's crazy . . . Do you remember the first time you actually took part in political activity?

GS: I got into political action when I was fourteen or fifteen, at the time of the national campaign by *lycée* students against the law brought in by the defence minister Michel Debré in 1973, which ended the deferment of national service for university students. The following year, we protested against planned education reforms. Every year, the government seemed to dream up a new project which, as soon as spring arrived, would invariably have the students out in the streets! To tell the truth, at the beginning I was just following the others, but then I began to really get into it. I threw myself into my apprenticeship as a political activist with great enthusiasm: strikes, demonstrations, meetings at the labour exchange, 'counter-lessons' taught by students, endless discussions . . .

AA: Where did you fit on the political spectrum?

GS: On the left, and even to the left of the left. I wasn't a member of any particular party or movement, but I felt a vague affinity with Michel Rocard's PSU (Unified Socialist Party), which I saw as being somewhere between Alain Krivine's Communist Revolutionary League and the traditional PS (Socialist Party). Intellectually speaking, I was on the same wavelength as the *Nouvel Observateur*, and greatly admired the magazine's co-founder, left-wing journalist Jean Daniel.

AA: More generally, what was your vision of the world? Had you travelled much?

GS: I'm sad to admit that it was rather narrow. My parents' geographical horizons were limited; as a family, our tradition was always to spend our holidays in the village of Mazuby in the eastern Pyrenees. The only border we would ever cross was the one between France and the principality of Andorra to buy pastis and cigarettes for my parents and records and cassettes for me. When I was about fifteen or sixteen, I discovered a passion for rock music, everything from Chuck Berry to David Bowie, taking in the Beatles,

Bob Dylan, Janis Joplin, Jimi Hendrix, Pink Floyd and Led Zeppelin along the way ... I expressed my sense of freedom, my yearning to be somewhere else, through music. Rock allowed me to assert my own identity, but also to start dreaming of freedom and independence. In Béziers or Mazuby, out in rural France, I was listening to the American dream! Strangely, though, I didn't have the desire or the courage to go any further and see London or the States for myself. My rebellion took place solely inside my head.

The Mediterranean: the Mother Sea[17]

AA: Up until that time, had you always lived in the south of France?

GS: Yes, ever since my birth in Sète, on 11 May 1957, under the Fourth Republic ... That seems so far away now! I was born in the rue Paul-Valéry, just next to the *lycée* which also bears this famous poet's name. There's a wonderfully hopeful symbolism in being born under the auspices of this great thinker who was so inspired by the Mediterranean, the sea which flows through my veins as it does through yours,

17 The phrase used here ('*La Mère Méditerrannée*', literally 'The Mother Mediterranean') draws its meaning from the similarity between the words for 'sea' (*mer*) and 'mother' (*mère*), which are both pronounced identically in French. Many writers have used this evocative expression to refer to an ancient shared Mediterranean cultural heritage which transcends the divisions imposed by modern notions of national and ethnic 'difference'.

Azdyne. How could anyone forget Sète, with its rocky spur jutting defiantly out towards the horizon.

AA: It's a magnificent town, that's for sure. No one who was born on its shores can ever forget the Mediterranean. It lives in us and soothes us. Did you live in Sète for long?

GS: Until I was eleven, in the very working-class 'upper district' (quartier haut). The town was built by immigrants, mainly from southern Italy. A lot of fishing families came to live there in the nineteenth century. Although it was founded by Louis XIV, and has always been French – despite briefly falling into British hands in 1710 – this 'peculiar island', as Paul Valéry called the town, still has an Italian soul to this day. You can see this in the colours, as well as in the personality and family names of its inhabitants. When I was born, my parents were still finishing their studies. They were penniless and could only rent a small apartment. We lived frugally but we were happy, I think.

AA: Who were your parents?

GS: My father, Serge, was born in 1932 and came from a very modest background. His parents had met at the Établissements Fouga, a company founded in Béziers just after the First World War. At the time, this great French engineering firm, which produced equipment for the railway industry before moving into the aeronautical sector, was the pride of the region. My grandmother was a secretary and typist and my grandfather worked on the factory floor. His father, my great-grandfather, had walked into France from Andorra at the beginning of the twentieth century.

My grandmother on my mother's side had been a school-mistress in Sète, and had married the son of farmers from the Pyrenees, who was in the army. They had my mother, Mireille, quite late, fifteen years after her brothers and sisters. My grandfather, who died before my mother could really get to know him, had bought a little house in the village of his birth, which I've already told you about, and which has always meant a lot to me. We would spend whole summers up in this village perched a thousand metres above the Aude valley; that's where my passion for the mountains and hiking was forged.

After having to spend ten years living apart most of the time because of their postings as teachers, my parents were at last able to be together with me under one roof in Béziers in 1970. At the beginning, I didn't do very well in school because I had terrible handwriting ... proof if any were needed that I was born to be a doctor! Later on, my intellectual side came through more, and that's no doubt the reason I didn't have many friends. Living as we did in an Italian neighbourhood, the main avenues for socialising in my school were catechism classes and sport. Since my parents, both science teachers brought up on Darwinism, weren't religious, I didn't go to catechism. In some ways I regret not having received any religious education; I'm often bemused by other people's rituals and beliefs, and maybe I would be better able to understand them if I had been introduced to this side of things. As for sport, I did a bit of judo but wasn't very good and soon gave it up. My parents didn't push me: taking part in sports wasn't very high on the list of intellectual values in the 1960s. It was only much later that I got into running, with a bit more perseverance this time, as I'm over sixty now but still regularly running marathons.

AA: What did you read when you were young?

GS: Everything I could lay my hands on, but I had two favourite authors: Jules Verne, who fuelled my yearning for escape, and Émile Zola, who moved me with his portraits of Paris and his tales of social injustice, class struggle and human misery. It was through books that I forged my political culture.

AA: I also liked Zola a lot, especially *The Ladies' Paradise* (*Au Bonheur des dames*) – I was lucky enough to have worked on the TV adaptation of the novel.[18]

GS: Zola wrote about Paris, which I visited for the first time in September 1973. It was a great eye-opener for me and I immediately fell in love with the city. I could never have imagined at the time that it would become my adopted home, but also the tomb of one of my children. At that time, Paris was synonymous with life. And you, Azdyne, you were born on the other side of the Mediterranean, in Algeria, weren't you?

AA: Yes, in 1947, ten years before you. I come from Bône, which was renamed Annaba following Algeria's

---

18 Translator's note: the novel tells the story of an early Parisian department store and the vicissitudes faced by a young salesgirl from the provinces.

independence in 1962. Saint Augustine was born nearby, in Tagaste; he was a Berber – it's a great source of pride for us!

A charming port city five hundred kilometres from Algiers, Annaba was known as 'little Paris'. My father, himself a Berber, was born in 1898 and studied at the famous al-Azhar university in Cairo. Before meeting my mother, he had first been married to a French woman and opened a driving school in France, before moving to Egypt, and then on to Gaza, where he would become a theologian.

My mother, his second wife, was Egyptian, with Palestinian and Algerian roots. She was fifteen when she married my father, who was thirty-three. From their union, my fourteen brothers and sisters and I would be born in Egypt, Gaza and Algeria, where we would return following the creation of the state of Israel. Like me, my father had itchy feet . . .

GS: What was his profession?

AA: A rich landowner who was every bit the Ottoman *bey*, and who had taken lessons in religion from my father, left him some land in his will. From then on, my father decided that it was enough for him just to teach Arabic and religion, and we lived on very little. The form of Islam that he professed was moderate, and not concerned with passing judgement or preaching unquestionable precepts. Nor were any of my sisters made to wear the veil, which was pretty rare for a theologian's family.

Through his studies at al-Azhar, my father had acquired a certain prestige and contributed funds for the construction of the mosque, which, as I mentioned earlier, now bears his name. As you can tell, I consciously moved away from this family image of piety and parsimoniousness; I already thought of myself as an iconoclast! To tell the truth, I think I've spent the rest of my life rebelling against it . . .

GS: What memories do you have of your childhood?

AA: My parents died a long time ago and it all seems so far away for me now. To be honest, I felt a bit lonely surrounded by my ten sisters (the eleventh died) and my two younger brothers, while the brother I was closest to lived in Egypt. It was pretty crowded in our house and I didn't have many friends. The beach was where I could let off some steam, but what with French school and Koranic school, I didn't get much time to myself. I think that this was when I decided to reject both France and religion. The schoolmistresses would talk to us about politics, and I couldn't stand their colonialist discourse. The male teachers were all reservists in the French army and gave their lessons dressed in combat gear, and we had to sing the *Marseillaise* at the beginning of each term. At the madrasa, there was yet another set of precepts, and I couldn't get myself expelled . . . because the teacher was one of my father's disciples! Having to continually switch between the two felt a bit schizophrenic. It was later on, with the Algerian war and France's defeat and withdrawal, that my political consciousness would be born.

GS: You don't really talk about your mother, this Egyptian woman who brought up her many children in what was a foreign country for her.

AA: My mother was illiterate, and since she didn't speak the Algerian dialect, she was quite isolated. With fourteen children and the house to look after, she was completely run off her feet and didn't have a particularly close relationship with me, but she did like to sing, and those are my fondest memories of her. She used to sing versions of classic songs by the inimitable Egyptian diva Oum Kalthoum. These memories certainly contributed to my later love of Egypt. Looking back, my parents' story is that of millions of mixed marriages, which have always seemed to me to pose many difficulties.

GS: Mixed marriages? But your parents were both Muslims, weren't they?

AA: Yes, but the way I see it, a mixed marriage involves two nationalities, two different identities. It's true that the *Ummah*, the community of all Muslims, is wide and diverse, but I still don't think that it's a straightforward business for an Algerian to marry an Egyptian. My mother always remained an Egyptian immigrant in Algeria and she never really integrated into local life, I'm sorry to say. And I think that you would see the same differences between two Algerians if one had been born in France and the other in Algeria.

GS: What about the situation of Jews in Algeria?

AA: I already had my doubts about France and I also became mistrustful regarding Jewish people. I found it hard to accept what had been done to the Palestinians in 1947 with the establishment of Israel and the wars which followed. Then, like many Algerians, I saw the choice made by some

Jews to take French nationality following independence in 1962 as an act of betrayal.

GS: It's clear that at that time, Azdyne, you shared that particular form of antisemitism which is far too common in the Arab and Muslim world, by which Jews, as a group, are blamed for political choices which they do not necessarily agree with as individuals, and for which they bear no responsibility.

The split between Algerian Jews and Muslims can be traced back to the Crémieux Decree of 1870, which gave automatic French citizenship to the 'Israelite natives' of Algeria, in order to shift the demographic balance within the French colony.[19] This wasn't something that the Jewish community had asked for, but simply a decision taken by the French government. In 1962, they had little choice but to leave Algeria, caught as they were between the FLN on the one hand, and the OAS on the other.[20]

AA: I didn't quite see things in such black and white terms,

---

19 Translator's note: conquered by France in 1830, Algeria was declared part of France in 1848 and administered as four French departments. However, French nationality was only granted to European settlers. Algerian Muslims had the status of '*indigènes*' and possessed limited civil and legal rights.

20 Translator's note: the FLN (*Front de Libération Nationale*, National Liberation Front) was formed in 1954 to campaign and fight for Algeria's independence from France. Its armed wing was the ALN (*Armée de Libération Nationale*). The OAS (*Organisation Armée Secrète*, Secret Army Organisation) was a right-wing paramilitary group founded in 1961 by French army officers opposed to President Charles de Gaulle's moves to grant Algerian independence. It carried out a campaign of bombings and assassinations in Algeria and mainland France.

even at the time: I've always greatly admired some Jews, like Henri Alleg, the journalist who exposed the French army's use of torture in Algeria, Maurice Laban, who campaigned for independence, or Pierre Ghenassia, who sacrificed his life for Algeria.[21] My views have also been changed by people that I've met, such as my Arabic teacher in Jordan, who was Jewish, or my neighbour Richard in Drancy, whom I've already told you about and who was always a great friend to me, even after 13 November 2015.

GS: What memories do you have of the Algerian war?

AA: I was seven when the war started. I can remember hearing the sound of explosions from our classroom, that must have been around 1957, when I was ten. We didn't know whether it was the French or the Algerian guerrillas who were doing the bombing. When we came out of the gates of the French school, the poor Algerians, who couldn't read, would be waiting for us to read the newspaper for them.

I began handing out leaflets in the street calling for a Free Algeria. At school, they'd be telling me about the French Revolution, but outside, I was campaigning against the mother country ... to the extent that, in 1960, I was even 'imprisoned', aged just thirteen! You see, the older militants would use the younger ones, as they would only be held in the cells for a few hours. I still felt that I had been the victim of a great injustice, and as soon as I was let out, I

---

21 Translator's note: Pierre Ghenassia was a Jewish Algerian student who joined the ALN as a medical orderly. He was killed in battle in 1957, aged seventeen.

began handing out leaflets for the FLN again. How could it be a crime to defend the independence of one's country?

Seeing that I was on the verge of having to repeat my final-year classes for a third year running, my father sent me to live with a cousin in Constantine. It was my first real journey, five hours by bus from our home, and I was finally free of Koranic school! I stayed there for two years and got to know our cousin, who was an educated, cultured man employed as a manager in a company run by a Frenchman, who would often come round to the house for a drink. Here was a good man, in whose presence the war no longer seemed so clear-cut for me. Every week, my cousin would bring home records by Middle Eastern artists singing Egyptian classics which reminded me of my mother: Abdel Halim Hafez, Oum Kalthoum, Asmahan, Farid El-Atrache ... He introduced me to the cinema, gave me pocket money and, for the first time in my life, I could buy sweets and eat fresh bread. As the nineteenth-century writer Chateaubriand so brilliantly put it: 'Oh money, that I have scorned so greatly and still cannot bring myself to love, no matter how I try, I am forced to confess that you do have some merit: source of freedom, you make possible a thousand things in our existence, where everything is difficult without you!'[22]

---

22 '*Oh! argent que j'ai tant méprisé et que je ne puis aimer quoi que je fasse, je suis forcé d'avouer pourtant ton mérite: source de la liberté, tu arranges mille choses dans notre existence, où tout est difficile sans toi.*' François-René de Chateaubriand, *Mémoires d'outre-tombe* (1849)

'I could have turned bad'

GS: What profession did you want to go into?

AA: I loved football, but I couldn't see myself building my life around it. All told, I've worked in over ten different professions, in business, sport and the cinema, as I've told you before. And it's not over yet! I've always been a jack of all trades. In this sense, I admire Leonardo da Vinci, the archetype of the universal genius, who also drew inspiration for his flying machines from the Berber scholar Abbas ibn Firnas. Born in Andalusia in the year 810, this inventor, who was also a doctor, a chemist and an engineer, was the first person to think seriously about how man could fly. What greater symbol could there be of the unity which exists between East and West?

As well as thinking about a future career, I already felt an urge to travel at that age. I hopped around all over the place. When I was fourteen, my father took me to Egypt to visit one of my brothers who was living there. But I was rebellious and didn't want my future to be decided so abruptly. So my father found a means of getting me out of the way by sending me to Jordan to live with an uncle.

I duly took a Royal Jordanian Airlines flight from Cairo to Amman, on 3 September 1962. I felt guilty about my treatment of my parents, as I'd given them a very hard time, but my freedom was too precious to me. I ended up staying in Jordan for four years, until the age of eighteen.

GS: Did you continue to rebel during those years?

AA: Yes, and I could have turned bad. But at school, I met a Jewish teacher of Arabic who greatly inspired me and opened my eyes to the world. He was a Samaritan, blond with green eyes, and descended from the Israelites, but nevertheless opposed to the policy of conquering Arab lands pursued since 1947. Thanks to him, I came to understand the complexity of the Arab world. He was a real-life good Samaritan! In Jordan, the Palestinian issue was ever-present, and I was particularly interested in this because of my association with the Algerian liberation struggle. The Palestinian refugees in Jordan hoped that they would be able to follow a similar path to freedom.

The clearest memories that I have of the 1960s, though, involve beer and rock music! It was in Jordan, Jerusalem to be precise, that I first drank alcohol and discovered John Lennon, The Shadows, Elvis Presley, Cliff Richard, Neil Diamond ... The cinema, and Egyptian cinema in particular, also helped open my eyes to the world.

GS: Just like me, then, with the film club in Béziers that I was telling you about. As I didn't have any opportunities to travel outside my provincial microcosm, cinema was a window on culture, life and the outside world. Two films left a particularly strong impression on me because of what they had to say about racism: *Dupont Lajoie* (*The Common Man*) by Yves Boisset, from 1975, which uses its depiction of a murder to denounce the cowardice of human beings and their everyday racism, and *Ali: Fear Eats the Soul* by Rainer Werner Fassbinder, a more subtle work. That, and the fact that the cinema was where you could hold girls' hands in the dark!

AA: Haha! For my part, I remember seeing *The Battle of Algiers* by Gillo Pontecorvo, which definitely reminded me of what I had lived through in Algeria during the 'events': demonstrations, bombings, the French paras ... Didn't this passion for cinema inspire you to consider it as a future career?

GS: The fact is, unlike you, I didn't have any artistic ambitions; I felt I was too clumsy. And then I had an excellent philosophy teacher in my last year of *lycée*, a communist with a passion for psychoanalysis, who gave me the idea of studying medicine, with a view to becoming a psychiatrist. My mother was delighted to think that I would be following in the footsteps of her older brother, although my father didn't seem so bothered.

AA: Were you a communist, like your teacher?

GS: No, I was extremely wary of the French Communist Party (PCF), as I was horrified by Stalinism and considered that the destalinisation process within the PCF had been completely inadequate.

AA: For my part, if we leave aside the Algerian war of independence, it was around the age of eighteen that I first began to take an active interest in politics. From Amman, I went to Syria in 1965, to study in Damascus, the capital of the Umayyads. Then, at the end of my grant, I headed to Cairo in 1966. At the time of the Six-Day War between Israel and the Arab states in June 1967, every weekend I would go with a group of about fifteen other students to the Suez

Canal to chant our support for the troops. I've got wonderful memories of those years in Cairo and the great feeling of solidarity between different communities (Kuwaitis, Algerians . . .). And I've always found Egypt interesting for its culture, particularly its cinema, but also for its politics, with its pan-Arab ambitions.

In 1968, aged twenty, I considered going to Vietnam with an Algerian friend to fight alongside the communists against the Americans. We took the boat from Alexandria to Beirut, but we ended up stopping in Syria, where we stayed for three months. After a frantic period spent shuttling around the Middle East, I ended up in Baghdad, the ancient capital of the Abbasid empire, then went on to Basra and Kuwait.

GS: What were you doing in all these different cities? What were you living off?

AA: I would be taken in by the Algerian community. I used to go out, drink, occasionally go to the mosque. In Kuwait, I received a grant to finish my secondary studies, but after I got a bit rowdy at a demonstration in the university, I got thrown out.

So I decided to go to France and start a new life. After passing through Rome, and then Geneva, I hitchhiked up to Paris, where I arrived in June 1969. Every time I walked down the Rue de l'École-de-Médecine, I would start dreaming of becoming a doctor, but all I could get were low-grade manual jobs. I didn't find the same level of solidarity between Algerians in Paris as in the Middle East. There's no two ways about it: life was hard. But I didn't really feel any racism at that time; when I went to the post office, I was even rather touched to see French people helping Algerians fill out forms. That was just one example. I felt there was a certain social cohesion, in spite of everything that had happened: the country had been divided, yet I never felt I was being judged.[23]

GS: You were beginning to forgive France?

AA: Yes, it was in Paris that I forgave France; French people there didn't seem unpleasant towards Algerians.

GS: That's surprising. I don't have the same memories as far as tolerance towards Algerian immigrants was concerned. In particular, I can remember a classmate being the victim of racist attacks, but maybe that had something to do with changing times, as this was in the 1970s.

AA: Yes, I think that mistrust and resentment really exploded with the policy of family reunion and the global economic crisis. So was the 1970s the decade when you became politicised?

GS: Yes, I first saw action in the strikes by *lycée* students, but it was at university that I became a 'card-carrying' activist. In my first year of medicine, I was too busy cramming for my exams to get closely involved, but I joined the National Union of French Students (UNEF) the following year. It

---

23 Translator's note: the post-war period and ensuing wars of independence (Indochina, Algeria) saw considerable political instability in France, and there was great bitterness among the one million French colonists ('*pieds-noirs*', literally 'black feet') who had been forced to leave Algeria and move to France, often penniless, following independence in 1962.

was in the student union movement that I discovered the sincerity, the commitment and, perhaps surprisingly because it's not the first thing one associates with them today, the open-mindedness of the communist students. It was in this context that I ended up joining the Union of Communist Students (UEC) in 1977. I felt that I was in direct contact with history, although I always retained a critical distance, particularly on the subject of the USSR.

AA: Did you ever go there, to the 'other side' of Europe?

GS: No, I didn't feel the need to. Some of my friends went to Poland or the German Democratic Republic; they were full of praise for the access to culture, education and housing, but at the same time they were aware of the absence of free speech and, among the people, a desire for 'Western-style' consumption.

I only went to the USSR much later, in 1987, when Mikhail Gorbachev was president. The Franco–Soviet Association had decided to assemble five hundred French citizens to visit the USSR and observe events, and I took part in this trip in my capacity as public health physician for the Hautes-Pyrénées department. I met with Muscovites, visited a psychiatric hospital, some factories, and Star City – where I shook hands with the first woman cosmonaut, Valentina Tereshkova – and at the end we were received in the Kremlin by Gorbachev himself. An amazing wind of freedom was blowing across Moscow.

AA: As communist sympathisers, we both have a degree of shared history. In Paris, I myself had begun getting interested in the PCF and supporting certain political causes. At the end of 1969, with 20 francs in my pocket, I made my way to West Berlin, the city at the heart of the great geopolitical struggles of the Cold War. I would spend a year there, staying with a woman who – I would later realise – worked on the streets.

GS: You mean that she was a prostitute?

AA: Yes, this was West Berlin at the end of the 1960s, among people who were more or less on the margins of society. At that time, I was to some extent living outside most moral, or even legal, conventions. For instance, I tried to enrol at university using a doctored *baccalauréat* certificate, without success. So I fell back on doing a bit of business between West and East Berlin, before getting sick of it and going back to Paris.

It was there, at the beginning of the 1970s, that I met the French communists. Having been impressed by the support given by the PCF to immigrants, I followed the rise of Georges Marchais, who fascinated me as a political personality.[24] I went to one of his public meetings at the Parc des Princes where, for the first time in my life, I sang not only 'The Internationale', but also the *Marseillaise* with pride and joy in my heart. The PCF's positions in favour of women and their freedom, and the contraceptive pill, along with its anti-racist and anti-colonialist stance, particularly appealed to

---

24 Translator's note: Georges Marchais (1920–1997) was a former mechanic who led the PCF from 1972 to 1994.

me. It was thanks to the PCF, in fact, that I read *La Question*, Henri Alleg's famous book on the use of torture during the Algerian war.

GS: Alleg also wrote a history of the Algerian war and *Red Star and Green Crescent*, which looks at the Soviet republics of central Asia. According to him, this region was where the future of communism and Islam would be decided. It would be interesting to read it again in the light of the current situation ...

I think that the PCF can take full credit for keeping alive the memory of these painful questions around the Algerian war. I'm thinking, for example, of the murder in 1961 of Maurice Audin, the communist mathematician who worked as an assistant lecturer at the University of Algiers and was a supporter of the Algerian independence struggle.

AA: That's true, and it was the communists who tried to shine fresh light on these taboo subjects which the post-independence amnesty law had covered with a veil of secrecy. For a while, the memory of the events of the war and torture in particular had disappeared from everyone's radar.

GS: These debates are still raging today, with the opening up of the archives and the work of historians like Benjamin Stora. It was a traumatic period for France and a traumatic period for Algeria, which we are still paying for to this day.

AA: In my view, the Algerian war is one of the most significant events of the past seventy years, for Algeria, obviously, but also for France. Did people talk about it in your family when you were a child?

GS: I don't remember hearing anything, but it's probably because my memory doesn't go back that far: the wars which formed part of my childhood memories are the Vietnam War, on the television and in my parents' conversations, and the Second World War, in the stories told by my grandparents.

AA: Yet the Algerian war and the wave of Algerian immigration which followed have had enormous consequences. French society has been changed by them, there's no denying it, as has political life. My life, my wife, my children – all of it has been a tale of two countries.

3

'Now that youth . . .'

GS: So, on the night of 13 November 2015, our son Clément called at about one in the morning. He'd been watching the live reports on the news channels and trying in vain to get through to Lola on her mobile, and had waited as long as he could before letting us know. When it was announced on the TV that the police assault on the Bataclan had finished, that the survivors were able to get out and the wounded were being evacuated, the lack of response from Lola began to take on a different meaning.

Right at that moment, though, neither Clément, Emmanuelle nor I could bring ourselves to think that the worst might have happened, or even consider its likelihood. We clutched at the statistics; they were talking about several dozen deaths – this initial figure was a bit of an under-estimate compared to the final tally. Out of a total of about 1,500 concertgoers in the Bataclan, there was a greater chance that she would be among the survivors than among the dead. She might have lost her phone in the crush, or perhaps she was too shocked to answer our calls? Or even wounded? This was the worst scenario that we were prepared to consider for the moment . . . We just hoped that she hadn't been injured too seriously.

Our second son, Guilhem, who lived nearby, soon came to join us. He arrived in tears and we could see that he didn't share our optimism, or rather our denial. We made an effort to reassure him, and reassure ourselves. To tell him that there was still hope. Then we turned on the television, where the images of police and paramedics, lit by blue flashing lights, were playing on a loop. An emergency number was scrolling across the bottom of the screen and we called it, once, ten times, a hundred times, right through the night . . . We kept getting the same message: 'The number you are trying to call is busy, please try again. The number . . .' That's when I decided to put out a call on Facebook and Twitter. Quite soon, the people looking for news of their loved ones had come together under the hashtag #Rechercheparis (#Searchingparis). Desperate messages from families and friends filled our computer screen, along with photos of Lola and many other missing people, almost all of them youngsters. This internet page was the most desperate place on Earth. Sometimes, there would be a message announcing a happy outcome: such or such a person had been found in casualty, or at the police station, giving a statement. Each time this happened, it gave us fresh hope – surely it's going to be the same thing with Lola – but also fresh disappointment – when is it going to be our turn? When will be able to breathe a sigh of relief?

I received dozens, hundreds of messages of support ('I'm praying for you'), offers of help ('My cousin's a nurse at hospital x or y, she'll make enquiries) and requests for news ('So, Monsieur, have you found your daughter yet?'). Many were well intentioned, but they did rather get in the way as we had to sort through them, looking for the message which might contain a real piece of information. And this message never came.

There was a brief moment of hope when someone indicated that Lola was safe on Facebook using the function which had been set up specially by the site. But this hope quickly faded, as it turned out that the person had clicked on it accidentally, and had quickly deleted the post. I finally got through to the famous hotline at around five in the morning, but the operator said she had no information regarding Lola. She directed us to the call centres for the *Assistance publique-Hôpitaux de Paris* (AP-HP, Public Assistance for Hospitals in Paris), the military hospitals (Percy, Bégin), Delafontaine hospital in Saint-Denis, the inter-district hospital in Créteil ... and the Forensics Institute, where the bodies would be taken. Emmanuelle and I called all the different hospitals, each time getting the same reply: 'No, your daughter is not on any of our lists, but there are a lot of wounded people who still haven't been identified. We advise you to call back later.'

Finding Lola, the unbearable wait

GS: We reasoned that if Lola was wounded, unconscious, or had lost her identity papers, we needed to provide the hospital with a description which would allow her to be identified. So Emmanuelle gave a description of Lola's distinguishing features: she had two small tattoos, one of a slice of lemon, the other of a slice of lime on the inside and outside of her left ankle. But the call centre operator at the AP–HP said that she couldn't take down this information, as there was nowhere to put it in the computer system ... There were a lot of things like this that no one had thought of.

Gradually, our apartment began filling up with people. My son, Clément, and his partner Amélie had come to join us; they were followed by Agathe, Lola's flatmate and her partner, Mallory, along with other friends of Lola's. During the morning, although we really didn't want to, we called the Forensics Institute, who said that they couldn't give out any information before the police identification unit had arrived. 'What time are they arriving? – I don't know, probably late morning.' When I called back as instructed: 'They haven't arrived yet, try in the early afternoon.' In the early afternoon: 'They haven't arrived yet, it'll be this evening, maybe even tomorrow.'

I couldn't bear the thought of spending a second night not knowing what had happened to Lola. We needed to mobilise the media and make sure that providing information to the families became a priority. So I called a journalist friend,

Claude Guibal, and with her help gave radio interviews to RTL, France Inter and other stations. During the afternoon, there were messages on Facebook and Twitter saying that a reception and support centre was being set up at the Military School near the Eiffel Tower. I tried checking this information on the ministerial websites, but couldn't see any official confirmation. So we decided to go to the emergency department at the Georges-Pompidou European Hospital (HEGP), where Mallory had a contact and where, rumour had it, there were still some wounded people who had yet to be identified. As we were driving in the car beside the Seine, Mallory checked his smartphone. A mobile number had been posted on Twitter for people to call for news regarding Lola. The people who called it were being told that she was dead. Messages of condolence were also beginning to appear on social media, only to be quickly retracted. The person who had given out this information was someone working for a voluntary organisation, not an official; we thought it was just an internet troll and decided to continue on to the hospital. On arrival at HGEP, we were met by the psychiatric team. They informed us that all the wounded had been identified and that Lola was not on the list.

It was at that moment that all hope left me. It was a weird feeling; I no longer expected to see her again, but I still had no confirmation of her death either. I found myself unable to think. We left the hospital and, rather than going to the Military School, where it had in the meantime been confirmed that the reception centre was now set up, we decided we would rather go home, where we would be surrounded by our friends, in order to call that dreaded number.

AA: Georges, I just can't speak ... And that wait – so inhuman. I didn't know that you had to go through such torment before learning the terrible news.

GS: When I got home, I dialled the number, and it was Stéphane Gicquel, the general secretary of Fenvac (*Fédération nationale des victimes d'attentats et d'accidents collectifs*, National Federation for Victims of Terror Attacks and Disasters), who answered. Although he was a representative of a voluntary organisation, he was still part of the Foreign Ministry's emergency response team at the Quai d'Orsay. He told me the same thing as he had to those who had called him previously. It was over. As I wanted to be absolutely sure, I asked for an official to call me back. Benoît Camiade, the head of the victims' support service at the Ministry of Justice, duly confirmed the news to me with great courtesy, humanity and competence, for which I would like to thank him, even if this could do nothing to lessen the shock. I broke down. It was over ... Lola was gone for ever.

Then, like in a bad film, the phone rang again. The Forensics Institute were calling to get some information about Lola: height, weight, hair colour, piercings, tattoos ... as if she hadn't yet been identified. A doubt had just begun to creep into my mind when, a few moments later, I received another call, this time from the police: 'We deeply regret to have to inform you of the death of your daughter. – Thank you, we've already been informed. Could you coordinate with your colleagues, please?' Announcing the death to anonymous callers, before informing the parents by telephone, with repeated calls, in fits and starts ... The process was the absolute model of how not to do things. This was the epilogue to a frenzied, exhausting, inhuman day of searching.

The following days

AA: What happened over the following days?

GS: The calm after the storm. I can remember how stunned I felt in the mildness of that Indian summer in Paris. The next morning, 15 November, like every Sunday, I went running with my friends from the athletics club in the Bois de Vincennes park. They all knew what had happened, of course; they understood completely why I needed to run, and they surrounded me with all the warmth that I needed.

When I got back home, I turned on the radio and heard the journalist Philippe Meyer on France Culture reading some verses taken from a poem by Louis Aragon: 'Now that youth / Breathes its last breath upon the blue-tinged pane / Now that youth / Has betrayed me with mechanical disdain ...'[25] Unlike some of his less thoughtful colleagues, he had not seen fit to react to the horror of what had happened

---

25 '*Maintenant que la jeunesse s'éteint au carreau bleu / Maintenant que la jeunesse / Machinale m'a trahi ...*'

with glib, off-the-cuff declarations. Poetry is a refuge in the face of barbarity. It made me cry, and those tears did me a lot of good.

On Monday 16 November, in the late afternoon, we went to see Lola's body at the Forensics Institute, on Quai de la Rapée, a sinister red-brick building beside the Seine, imprisoned within a constant flow of traffic. Mallory and Agathe accompanied us as we passed through these Stations of the Cross: through the security check at the corner of the Pont d'Austerlitz, a halt beneath the tents housing the medical and psychological emergency units, another wait under a second tent, the reception at the entrance to the building, through to the counter to fill in a form, another waiting room, before going through into yet another room deep in the bowels of the Institute. We were unable to think, take decisions, answer questions; we were asked if we needed a medical statement to be signed off from work, we replied that we didn't, which meant that we had to come back during the week to get one. After a long time spent waiting, a psychologist came to prepare us. I must say that she did so with a precision and a professionalism that we greatly appreciated, whereas other parents later reported negative experiences of this process to me. 'You are going to see your daughter behind a glass screen; you won't be able to touch her. Her body is covered with a sheet. Her face is intact, her mouth is a little bit open. Her expression is calm, but her face is very red, as no embalming has been carried out and your daughter was lying on her stomach for a long time on the floor of the Bataclan.' When we went in, the reality corresponded exactly to this description, apart from the fact that her face didn't look all that red to us. She seemed to be sleeping, and even ready to wake up if we'd insisted a bit. We all broke down but, strangely, passing through this stage also made us feel better. The serenity of her expression allowed us, and still allows us to imagine today that maybe she didn't see death coming, that she was too busy dancing to the music.

AA: It's all so hard. How did you get through this time?

GS: In the days that followed, our tight family circle was broken, on the one hand by the media 'invasion' – which we consented to at the beginning, then quickly (albeit temporarily) fended off – but also by the presence, this time very welcome, of our and Lola's friends.

I myself had contacted the press on 14 November, while we were still looking for Lola, in order to speak out about how long things were taking. I was trying to find a way of shaking up the authorities so that the families would be informed more quickly. But once this Pandora's box was opened, the telephone continued to ring even after the announcement of our daughter's death. I was reluctant at first, then took the decision to respond to the requests from the press; I knew that the media had a short attention span and this moment would soon pass.

I wanted to use these microphones that were being pointed towards me to put across two messages. The first was directly connected to what we had just been through: the system for identifying victims and informing families had serious shortcomings that urgently needed to be rectified, and I was prepared to help with this. The second message was more political: I wanted people to know that a purely security-oriented response involving police and military action alone would not satisfy me, and that it was necessary to search out and eradicate this problem at its root. I feared that France would be tempted to turn in on itself in hatred, or give in to calls for war, as the United States had done after 9/11. I thought it was important to say this as a victim, as a father who had just lost his daughter, and I was not the only one to speak out in this way. We 'took control of the pitch', to use a footballing metaphor, and I think that we played a part in ensuring that France reacted in a generally cool-headed manner faced with this terrible situation. The journalists who contacted me were aware that they were dealing with a grieving family and were careful in their choice of words with us, but after several days our family – and particularly my wife Emmanuelle – couldn't take any more of their incessant phone calls and filming at our house. So I stopped giving interviews and our pain went back to being an intimate affair among our family and friends for a couple of weeks, which seemed all too short.

Despite this, in the days and weeks which followed 13 November, people would be dropping by at the house almost every day. Everything was in a permanent state of improvisation: we didn't know who would be turning up, how many of them there would be, when they were coming. A lot of visitors brought food with them, but if there wasn't enough, we would go down and buy a bit more or order some pizzas. We would stick tables together, squeeze up on the sofa, sit on cushions or eat standing up ... We were all terribly sad and yet, it was somehow wonderful. Little by little, this period came to an end, but out of it came a whole circle of friends and a new feeling of conviviality, which we have kept ever since. Friendship had become a priority.

AA: Lola had a lot of friends, then?

GS: Yes, her friendships were an essential part of her life. Her many groups of friends, from every background imaginable, came to see us at the time of her death and we have continued to keep in touch since. Until the end, she had kept her friends from the *lycée* Hélène-Boucher, in the 20th *arrondissement*, where she had studied for her *baccalauréat*. There was also the group from her degree class at the ESSCA business school, including Julien, her first boyfriend; there were friends from her master's in publishing at Paris Sorbonne University; others knew her from her time spent in French-speaking Canada and Japan, and there were also her colleagues and friends from the publishers Éditions Gründ.

AA: Éditions Gründ, whose offices are just upstairs from where we're sitting now ... It must be hard for you to speak to me here, on the premises of Éditions Robert Laffont, who belong to the same group. Next to the lift, I saw the sign for Éditions 404, which Lola created.

GS: Yes and no; I like to be in this work environment which she loved so much.

AA: Did Lola always want to go into publishing?

GS: No, she took a bit of a circuitous route to get there. At high school, she always got very good marks. But at *lycée,* from the age of fifteen onwards, she was less focused, less interested in school, probably more interested in living life as a teenager. When she was in her final year of school, specialising in economics and science, a careers advisor steered her in the direction of a prestigious private business school, and she passed all the post-*baccalauréat* entrance tests that she sat.[26] How did she manage this? Because these tests are above all designed to assess students' ability to work in a group, and this was Lola's strong suit. So she went to study at the *École supérieure des sciences commerciales* in Angers, in central France, but business turned out not to be her cup of tea. She described her studies as a form of 'rigid training for aggressive capitalists'! However, it was in Angers that she met her boyfriend Julien, with whom she lived for five years, before breaking up with him.

AA: Did you pass on your love of reading to her?

GS: I certainly did, particularly Émile Zola: most of all she loved his novel *Nana* and its eponymous heroine. The story of Nana, this woman prepared to do anything in order to succeed, using her body if necessary, must have struck a chord with Lola; as a feminist, among other reasons, as the novel

26 Translator's note: after the *baccalauréat* exam, French students have the choice of going to a publicly run university or a specialised private '*école*'. The latter are much more expensive but offer better employment prospects post-graduation.

depicts the condition of women, objects of men's desire, and the ability of some women to emancipate themselves.

Like me, who dreamed of the world described by Jules Verne, Lola was also inspired by *The Mysterious Island*, a book which truly is an invitation to travel the world – an invitation she would later grasp with both hands – and which I used to read to the children in Egypt, one chapter at a time, each evening at bedtime. She also loved the Harry Potter books, fantasy, graphic novels and manga. Like her brother Guilhem, she liked drawing, and while studying in *lycée* she produced some drawings for an autobiographical graphic novel.

It was while studying for her degree that she turned towards publishing. During her studies at ESSCA, she did a work placement at Éditions Playback, and then another one with Gründ. After doing her master's in publishing at the Sorbonne, she spent six months working in Montréal on a placement with Les Éditions de l'Homme, who offered to take her on, but she wanted to come back to her hometown, Paris. I've wondered whether, if she'd accepted that job offer in Quebec . . .

AA: . . . things might have been different.

GS: Yes. Especially seeing as she had a burning desire to travel, to move around. She also went to Japan to study for a term at Sophia University in Tokyo, to Korea, to Cyprus, to the United States, around Europe . . . She came back from each of her trips with lasting friendships, which we have inherited from her, as if her life were being prolonged through them. I'm thinking of Pablo, who came back from Tokyo for Lola's funeral, and has recently invited us to his wedding in Mexico. And so many others . . . She had friends from every possible background, every kind of people; she took them for who they were.

Her women's roller derby team was called '*La Boucherie de Paris*' ('The Paris Butchers') and the players were '*bouchères*' ('butches'). This play-on-words tells you exactly what the sport is like – funny, irreverent, spectacular and strongly influenced by LGBT culture. Lola wasn't a lesbian herself and she never judged anyone; she loved people in all their diversity.

Even though the victims of the attacks are too often described as 'martyrs' – when they didn't set out to sacrifice themselves and weren't necessarily without their faults – I can easily imagine that Lola would be capable of feeling compassion for her killers.

AA: What was your reaction during the days that followed, as the investigation gradually revealed various details about the terrorists?

GS: It was hard for me to think about anything other than Lola's death, to be honest. Although my memories of those days are a bit vague, I know that I followed the news, even if this was just so as to be able to give a relevant reply to questions from journalists. In particular, I remember the coverage of the police operation on 18 November in Saint-Denis, during which Abdelhamid Abaaoud, presumed to be the logistical organiser of the attacks on the 13th, was killed.

I also saw the tragi-comic interview with Jawad Bendaoud on BFM TV and his arrest.[27]

AA: You amaze me. You never admit defeat. In this tragic situation, you take action, you keep moving, you appear in the media. Did you stop work, all the same?

GS: I kept myself busy, filling my time with one thing or another. I took a few days off to attend the congress of the French Society for Health and Environment (SFSE), on 24 and 25 November. There were a couple of reasons for this. At the time I was, and still am, an administrator for the SFSE, and I had played an active role in organising this congress. 2015 was a particularly important year as it coincided with the COP 21, the global conference on climate change which would result in the Paris Climate Agreement – signed by the majority of UN member states until the withdrawal of the United States on the orders of Donald Trump. As a satellite event of the COP 21 conference, the theme of our congress was: 'Climate change and health: what are the risks? what are the remedies?' and I had prepared a presentation which was already included in the programme. And I also think that I needed to 'ground myself' again, get back into a work routine which would let me escape the thoughts that were assailing me.

---

27 Translator's note: Jawad Bendaoud was convicted of providing shelter to two participants in the 13 November attacks, Abdelhamid Abaaoud and Chakib Akrouh. During the police raid on the flat where Abaaoud and Akrouh were hiding (during which both were killed), Bendaoud was giving a broadcast interview, and he himself was arrested on live television.

AA: Was this before the funeral and the national tribute for the victims?

GS: Yes, they only took place on 27 November. A drawn-out finale which would bring this section to a close. Early that morning, we had to go to the Forensics Institute to witness the removal of Lola's body. As we waited for the doors to open, we stood there, huddled against the eastern door of the Institute, which looks upstream over the Seine. The weather had changed since the 13th; it was a cold, foggy morning as you often get in Paris in winter. Above our heads, the metro viaduct was shrouded in mist and, from time to time, a train would burst forth from the Gare d'Austerlitz to punch its way through this cocoon of cloud. I remember being struck by the beauty of this spectacle, before raging against a world which dared to be beautiful at such a time.

AA: I'm so terribly sorry for these painful moments.

GS: That was the last day that I set eyes upon the body of my daughter. She was no longer behind a screen, but in an open coffin. Two weeks had passed since her death and time had done its work. Her face was no longer that of a girl sleeping peacefully. It was a corpse that I looked upon now, and upon which the coffin lid was closed.

Then we set off for the national tribute at Les Invalides. Emmanuelle, Clément, Guilhem, Mallory and I joined hundreds of other survivors and loved ones of the victims. It was cold. We stopped for a few minutes under the heated tent, set up between the building and its perimeter wall, a snug porchway where coffee and pastries were being served.

We then sat down in the stands, doing our best to keep out the cold using little blankets which had been handed out. The orchestra played Beethoven's Seventh Symphony while, in the courtyard, the Republican Guard, firefighters, police officers and hospital workers stood waiting for the president. Among them, the only face I could recognise was Patrick Pelloux, an emergency doctor, trade union activist and contributor to the satirical magazine *Charlie Hebdo*, whom I had seen on the TV like everyone else, but had also bumped into from time to time in meetings and for a radio programme, a few years back, where we had both talked about the heatwave of 2003. In front of us were victims' families and survivors; the ministers and other officials must have been sitting in the front row, but we couldn't see them. I can barely recall what François Hollande said. It was sober and short, thankfully. What I do remember is the silence that filled the courtyard of the Invalides and the music which covered this silence. Since childhood, I have always been sensitive to music, and two pieces particularly moved me that 27 November: the Jacques Brel song *'Quand on n'a que l'amour'* ('When you only have love'), sung by Camélia Jordana, Yael Naim and Nolwenn Leroy, and the sublime version of the *Marseillaise* played by the band of the Republican Guard. The voices of the three female singers, with Brel's lyrics and music, touched the depths of my heart, while the power of the *Marseillaise* in the orchestration by Berlioz echoed my determination to resist barbarity. Of course, Beethoven, Brel, Barbara and the *Marseillaise* weren't especially rock 'n' roll, and a more peevish listener might perhaps have bemoaned the absence of music more in tune with the tastes of the victims who had died at an Eagles of Death Metal concert.[28] Speaking for myself, I thought it was a fitting tribute, and anyway, that same afternoon we made some noise with folk and electric guitars beneath the dome of Père-Lachaise.

AA: It was at Père-Lachaise cemetery that you said your final goodbyes to Lola?

GS: That's right. It was a beautiful ceremony, and the speeches – moving and funny, just as I had imagined they would be – reflected the memory left by Lola in the hearts of those who had known her. The music sang out that day: her friends played some fantastic versions of songs, as well as pieces by Arcade Fire, David Bowie, T. Rex and Radiohead, which Lola loved. Before we went into the chapel, Marisol Touraine, the minister of health, and Anne Hidalgo, the mayor of Paris – who were my and Emmanuelle's employers, as at that time we worked for the Ministry of Health and the Paris city authority respectively – came to offer some words of sympathy. Then, along with the other personalities who were present, they attended the ceremony, participating discreetly in this moment of shared reflection. A great number of relatives, friends and colleagues were present and many

---

28 Translator's note: the singer-songwriters Jacques Brel (1929–1978) and Barbara (Monique Andrée Serf) (1930–1997) epitomise the tradition of classic French *chanson*, characterised by poetic lyrics and subtle, expressive vocals. As such they stand in contrast to the rhythmic dynamism and hedonism associated with rock music.

were unable to get into the domed chapel. In the cold and the silence, they waited outside for an hour, only able to hear muffled echoes from the ceremony. We then accompanied Lola's coffin to her grave. When I got back that evening, I posted a photo of the grave covered in flowers on Facebook, with the following commentary: 'Floods of love, song and laughter. A vibrant and moving ceremony today at Père-Lachaise. For Lola Salines and all the victims of murderous stupidity, in France and throughout the world. Thank you to all who were present and all who would have liked to be there.'

AA: It's so terrible, Georges. I am deeply sorry.

'Where is your son?'

GS: And for you, Azdyne, what happened after the attacks?

AA: Early in the morning of Monday 16 November, I noticed a whooshing sound, a noise I had heard before. Someone was trying to force my front door. A terrible racket followed, so I got up and saw a ray of light through the keyhole. I shouted: 'I'll let you in', but one of the men from the SWAT team yelled back: 'Police, hands up!' About ten policemen burst in and took Mouna and me back into our bedroom, while Maïssa, my youngest daughter who was still living with us, stayed alone in her room. They began turning the apartment inside out. At that moment, I didn't make the connection with Samy; I thought that he was still in Syria and, with checks at the borders, he couldn't get back into Europe.

We now know that he made his way into Europe via the Greek island of Leros, off the coast of Turkey. From Syria, he must have driven to Bodrum, in Turkey, to make the crossing to Leros using fake papers, and from there get to Hungary. At that time, the eastern European countries' borders were still like a sieve. What I also now know is that from 10 to 17 September 2015, the three attackers, including Samy, stayed in a hotel in Budapest. It was probably from there that Salah Abdeslam picked them up in his car to bring them back to Belgium. They then stayed in Brussels for almost a month and a half. But I only found this out later. The police quickly handcuffed the three of us and took us away separately to the offices of the General Directorate for Internal Security (DGSI) in Levallois-Perret, on the north-western edge of Paris.

GS: I'm finding it hard to believe that you still hadn't made the connection with Samy, but perhaps it seemed almost unthinkable, or even unacceptable to you, that, of all the jihadists out there, Samy would be involved in this horror.

AA: When we had spoken, and when I saw him in Syria, he had never mentioned anything whatsoever about preparing an attack. After I came back, we had occasionally had some news from Samy, but very little in the six months leading up to the tragedy. During this latter period, we came to realise that the replies to our messages were being written by his wife. She never said where he was, occasionally claiming that he was 'just next door with the cat'. We stopped believing her and assumed that he was either away fighting or ...

dead. Anyway, once I've been taken to the DGSI offices, they take off my hood. I'm on my own in a cell and don't know what's going on. Finally, a sergeant comes in:

'I'm going to show you some photos of people. Tell me if you recognise one.' I don't recognise any of them, apart from Samy.

'Yes, I recognise my son, Samy.' This was the famous photo that would appear in all the media. Some other officers then came in and put my diary from 2013, which they'd found on my desk, down on the interview room table.

'Do you recognise this object?'

'Yes, it's mine.' In the corner of one of the pages, I had written something which had attracted their attention: 'Salah, mission accomplished.' They thought this must be Salah Abdeslam, but I explained that it referred to an Algerian friend of mine called Salah, whom I'd helped find an apartment. There were also other things I'd noted down which they quizzed me about. They grilled me for four days, without any contact with another person, neither with my wife nor my daughter. I could imagine the fear that the girls must be feeling, but I knew that I had done nothing wrong.

GS: At what point, though, did you begin to realise that there might have been a link between Samy and the Bataclan?

AA: One of the interrogators asked me where my son was, and I replied: 'You probably know better than me, he's in Syria.' Then they put me in front of the Public Prosecutor and the conversation continued.

'For what purpose did he go to Syria?'

'Like the other youngsters, he went out to help the Syrians, or for *jihad* ... I don't know.'

'What, you really don't know?!'

'Yes, he went to take part in *jihad*, unfortunately.'

'No, Monsieur Amimour, your son is dead.'

I broke down. I made the connection with the attacks and repeated to myself over and over again that my son was dead, as if I was trying to understand what it meant. The judge then confirmed to me that Samy was one of the attackers involved in the massacre at the Bataclan.

I was unable to speak; I felt broken. The judge ended by saying: 'I will keep you in detention for another twenty-four hours. We'll talk about Syria.' They knew that I'd been there, as I'd said so in an interview I'd given with the newspaper *Le Monde* some time before on the subject of my journey to Syria.

GS: What did you feel after Samy's death was announced?

AA: The report by the parliamentary inquiry commission stated that Samy was identified on 15 November from his fingerprints. He was shot dead on the stage by a plain-clothes police officer from the BAC.[29]

I didn't shed a tear on learning this; I was somewhere between sadness, hatred, anger, fatigue and resentment. Above all, I was overcome by the thought of the ninety victims from the Bataclan and the forty others who died on the

---

29 Translator's note: the BAC (*Brigade Anti-Criminalité*) is a branch of the French national police which specialises in tackling urban crime. Its officers are not trained or equipped for dealing with terrorist incidents.

restaurant terraces. I don't know how Mouna got through these terrible times; we have never spoken about it since.

GS: You've never spoken about the announcement of your son's death? For me, that seems unbelievable!

AA: No, from that day on we've almost never spoken about Samy as a family. The subject is taboo. Over the following days, the investigators showed me the photos of the ten terrorists. I didn't recognise any of them. I didn't have a lawyer with me as they're not allowed to be present when suspects are being held and questioned for terrorism offences. We were finally released, my wife, my daughter and myself, on Friday 20th at midnight. In the taxi home, none of us spoke; there was absolute silence. And ever since that day, 20 November 2015, until we began the conversations that make up this book, we never spoke about 'that' again as a family.

A letter to my child

GS: What happened after this?

AA: After more than a month of bureaucratic wrangling, we were able to go to the Forensics Institute to see Samy. At the east door, an employee told us coldly which room he was in.

GS: This visit to the Forensics Institute is a terrible ordeal, which we've both been through, but I imagine that you must have felt that you were being looked at in a very different way by the people there than I did.

GEORGES SALINES & AZDYNE AMIMOUR

AA: I asked to be allowed in first, and I found my son covered with a white sheet. His head was shaved, and the look in his eyes when I had left him in Syria a year and a half earlier came back to me. Now, he was dead, inert, at the end of all that absurdity. I learned that he was shot at 9.57pm in the Bataclan, while I was watching the match. Mouna and Alya came in and joined me and, after saying a final goodbye, I kissed Samy on the forehead and screwed the coffin lid in place myself. That was the end of that.

GS: This corridor which leads to the east door of the Institute is where I came to find Lola. I imagine that everything was set up so that the victims' loved ones wouldn't come into contact with the families of the terrorists.

AA: That's right, the Forensics Institute had to deal not only with the one hundred and thirty victims, but also with the nine terrorists, who would be joined by their three accomplices, who died on 18 November in Saint-Denis. I imagine that this is why they put back the date of our visit several times before giving us the green light.

A hearse came to pick up Samy's body and we buried him after the cemetery had closed to the public. It was pitch black, no one had been informed of the date or time of the burial. I don't know what paradise looks like, but where we were that evening looked a lot like hell.

Samy's grave, which is unmarked, is in the Muslim section of the cemetery. The ceremony was simple, with a reading of verses from the Koran and the Muslim profession of faith. I was devastated that my son had gone so young, in the way he did, and that evening I thought a great deal about the victims. Back home, while Mouna and my daughters tried to comfort each other, I wrote a poem which came from the depths of my heart, and straight from the gut:

My beloved son, like ice, I am melting away.
I've travelled so far beneath this weight,
Your mother, your sisters and I, your friends too,
All telling the family of their memories of you.
At my age and in my health, on the road to Damascus,
Will I be able to find you at last?
Your French teacher, in her letter,
Said you were an angel for all those you met.
The day that I learned of your brutal death
From the mouth of some worthy, as cruel as a jackal,
And all those innocents who were not at war
In an instant were lying on the ground, dead.
And when one night I could think of nothing but you,
Your little cat Titisse cuddled up to me.
Seeing that I was stressed, strange, disturbed,
To comfort me she purred and purred.
I did not want all this and beneath the glare
of the press, the media and hateful stares
Will they be so quick to tar us all with the same brush,
Or use all this to crush our souls?
The people in charge promise us so much
And this violent world full of such
Injustice, when in fact we could

Live happily, stamp out evil, violence and hunger for good.
Here I stand, in front of your grave.
I recite a verse, mourn and go on my way.
How can I picture you? And your broken body,
Only Allah the Most High can judge you.[30]

GS: That's very moving, Azdyne, and you've really got talent. I feel sorrow for you and your family. I believe that extreme pain can bring out abilities that we didn't know we possessed, and that we must express our feelings, and not keep quiet. I also wrote a text, and I read these words out at Lola's funeral. It was in public, in front of a crowd,

---

30 *Mon fils bien-aimé, je fonds comme de la glace. / Tant de chemins suivis avec ma carapace, / Ta mère, tes sœurs et moi, et aussi tes amis, / Évoquent leurs souvenirs à toute la famille.*

Mon âge et ma santé, le chemin pour Damas / M'aideront-ils enfin à retrouver ta trace? / Ta prof de français, dans sa lettre, disait / Que tu étais cet ange à ceux qui t'ont croisé.

Le jour où j'ai appris cette mort brutale / Par la bouche d'un notable cruel, comme un chacal, / Et tous les innocents qui n'étaient pas en guerre / En un laps de temps se retrouvaient par terre.

Et lors d'une nuit je ne pensais qu'à toi, / Ton petit chat Titisse était collé à moi. / Me voyant stressé, bizarre et perturbé, / Pour me réconforter ne cesse de ronronner.

Je ne l'ai pas souhaité et sous les projecteurs / La presse et les médias et tous les détracteurs / Vont-ils enfin si vite cultiver l'amalgame, / Ou profiter de ça pour achever notre âme?

Tous les gouvernants qui nous promettent tant / Et toute cette injustice dans ce monde violent,

Alors qu'il est possible de vivre heureux enfin, / Éradiquer le mal, la violence et la faim.

Arrivé sur ta tombe, je me mets juste en face. / Je récite un verset, me recueille et je passe. / Comment t'imaginer? Et ton corps abîmé, / Seul Allah le Très Haut, lui, pourra te juger.

whereas you had to hide from the world. This is what I said on 27 November:

First of all, we are all gathered together here to think about Lola, but I also want us to think about the hundreds of other innocent people who have fallen victim to the same form of terrorism: in Paris, but also, in the past thirty days alone, at Sharm el Sheikh, in Beirut, in Bamako and in Tunis. Secondly, I want to say thank you for the hundreds of messages that I've received, that we've received since 13 November. The phrases which kept coming up the most in the emails, text messages and letters were probably: 'There are no words', 'I can't find words', 'I don't know how to express what I'm feeling' ... yet this admission of difficulty was more often than not followed by sensitive, delicate, intelligent, perfectly chosen words, which gave us great comfort. So, my third message is that we absolutely must not keep quiet. On the contrary, we have to speak to each other. And when we speak we mustn't just say that we love each other, even if that's important. We also have to try, together, to understand what is happening. 'The sleep of reason produces monsters' is inscribed on one of Goya's prints; we must not let reason go to sleep and, when necessary, we must wake it up. And if we do not have words, we can also express ourselves through images. Lola often did. I'm going to show you one of her drawings. It's probably not the best or the funniest one she ever did, but it really struck me when I saw it again in the past day or two, because in it she imagined her own grave. But don't worry, it was a joke grave, so fake, like the kids say. It had a cross on top for a start, and she knew that the real one wouldn't be like that. She drew this picture when she was writing up her master's dissertation. As she was having trouble keeping to the deadline, she did the obvious thing and starting doing little drawings instead of writing. I'm sure that this will bring back memories to anyone who's ever had to carry out this type of exercise. My fourth message is not to forget to laugh. Lola had an extra-large sense of humour. Her laugh was so joyful and sonorous that she could have a whole room collapsing in giggles. I really hope that we'll all laugh today, even though I can't promise you that there won't be any tears.

AA: That's so beautiful, Georges. Do you feel the need to go to Lola's grave often? With Mouna, we regularly go to the cemetery to see our child.

GS: I don't go often. When I go past Père-Lachaise, if I have the time, I look in to see how the grave is looking. It's just a very simple headstone, always covered with objects and flowers left by friends. We just had it engraved with a portrait of her done by her brother Guilhem, along with her name and the dates of her birth and death: Lola Salines: 06/12/1986, Tarbes – 13/11/2015, Bataclan. The engraved lines and the natural imperfections in the stone have moss growing on them; life reasserts its dominion, even in cemeteries.

The times when I find myself in front of her grave are also times for reflection. I don't talk to my daughter, but I do think about her. As far as I'm concerned, after death there is nothing. No afterlife, no reincarnation, no transmigration of the soul. But I do think that the people who have lived on this Earth have all left a mark by their passage; they live on for some time in the memories of those who knew them and they have their own eternal place within spacetime. My daughter exists no more today than she did before she was born, but she did live and, in a certain way, this reality is indelible. As the title of the book which she published with her fellow students at the end of her master's in publishing put it: *No one skis softly enough to leave no marks in the snow.*

Playing with death and losing

AA: Samy's grave is simple as well. Where is he today? I believe in resurrection and the journey of the soul after death. Every day, I ask my God that he might be forgiven and, my head hung in shame, I confess to you that he committed the greatest horror imaginable. Should I, *can* I even forgive him?

GS: 'Have you forgiven or would you consider granting forgiveness to your daughter's murderers?' This is a question often put to me, but one which I don't think makes much sense: they died without being judged. My forgiveness would no more help them than my eternal hatred would hurt them.

As Samuel Sandler, whose son and two grandsons were murdered by Mohammed Merah in front of their Jewish school in Toulouse in 2012, rather bluntly put it, 'If I'm going to ask myself whether I'm ready to forgive, first someone needs to ask me for forgiveness.' Indeed, the impossibility of such a conversation is one of the reasons underpinning my opposition to the death penalty.

AA: A few days after 13 November 2015, someone knocked at our door. It was a young guy from the neighbourhood coming to tell me that my son was a martyr and a hero. In his way, he wanted to share our pain and our grief, but was badly wrong in thinking that I saw things this way.

My son needed to be stopped before he killed any more people that night. On the other hand, if he had been sentenced to death – in a country where this is authorised – I would have been against it, as I'm opposed to the death penalty in general.

GS: As for me, I'm *totally* against the death penalty! Of course, the priority for the police was stopping the massacre, and to do that they had to kill the assailants, I can absolutely understand that; but I would have preferred them to have been apprehended alive, if that had been possible, and given long prison sentences. I'm against the irrevocable nature of the death penalty, which deprives us all of explanations. In a way, it shields the condemned person from the scrutiny and judgement of their victims. Once they are dead, I lose the ability to forgive them, but also the ability to withhold my forgiveness from them. The notion of forgiveness thus loses all meaning, and any possibility of redemption also disappears.

I'm not a Catholic, I'm not even a Christian, but I do believe that as long as a person is alive, they can still repent. I know that many people don't share this view, but personally I think that it's difficult to pass lifelong judgement on someone aged twenty-eight, as I doubt that the person in question would still be the same at sixty-eight. Besides, by killing a jihadist you're giving him the one thing he asks for: death as a martyr on the path to Allah.

AA: I would have preferred them to be put on trial and punished. The far-right terrorists Anders Breivik, who carried out the massacre in Norway in 2011, and Brenton Tarrant, who opened fire on mosques in Christchurch, New Zealand in 2019, were captured alive, and have therefore had to face their victims. In jihadist ideology, however, martyr-dom is so glorified that a killer will do everything in his power to himself be killed.

GS: In the United States, victims often think that the execution of their tormentors will bring them peace of mind, but things are far more complicated than that. Quite apart from the question of the death penalty, many victims of 13 November 2015 regret the fact that those directly responsible for the attacks were killed; they would have preferred them to be put on trial instead, in the hope, if nothing else, of getting some answers to their questions.

AA: Of the terrorists involved in the attacks of 13 November, Salah Abdeslam and his accomplices are still alive, and will be put trial in 2021. When I heard in the media that he was refusing to talk, I wondered whether, as the father of a jihadist, I should go and see him. Maybe he would be willing to talk to me. Who knows? If I could at least make myself useful by obtaining some information . . . I was the father of one of their own, and I can no longer talk to my son about what happened, in order to try to understand. I think that you can still say without shocking people that you remain, first and foremost, a father.

Maktoub

AA: In the face of the loss of a child, we are all helpless and, even if most people might disagree that our situations are comparable, the fact remains that you have lost your daughter, and I my son.

GS: I never imagined anything worse in life that losing a child. Lola was relatively adventurous, she took part in risky sports and often travelled alone. Looking at it objectively, there were sound reasons for us to be worried. Emmanuelle certainly was when Lola went sofa-surfing in Korea, for instance. Personally, I wasn't unaware of these risks, but I was sure that she herself felt that they were worth taking. I had an anxious mother, who held me back from following my adventurous impulses and who, above all, by not wanting to run any risks, ended up forgetting to live. By avoiding all risk, you expose yourself to the greatest risk of all: the risk of not living your life, and I didn't want to play out this same scenario with my own children.

AA: You're right: life is just a succession of risks. You have to live things to the full.

GS: Yes, we have to live, and living means taking risks. The philosopher Blaise Pascal wrote in his *Thoughts*: 'I have discovered that all the unhappiness of men arises from one single fact, that they cannot stay quietly in their own chamber.'[31] What else can you do? Lola got as much as humanly possible out of her all-too-short life, and that's a consolation to me. Yet the loss of a child registers extremely high on the scale of human suffering. It goes against the natural order of things; parents should as a matter of principle go first. As a parent, your job is to protect your offspring and, while you might be ready to give your own life to save your child, being unable to protect that child from death engenders a form of guilt. It's been hard for me not to think: 'And what if we'd stayed in the provinces? In Tarbes? In Martinique? Even in Egypt... Because in the end it was in Paris that Lola died.' But such speculation is pointless; what happened, happened.

AA: And yet, I know that you don't believe in destiny.

GS: That's right, nor in any idea of predetermination. We live in a chaotic, stochastic, quantum mechanical universe, where chance plays an enormous role. What happened on 13 November 2015 was determined by certain historical

---

31 *'Tout le malheur des hommes vient d'une seule chose, qui est de ne savoir pas demeurer en repos dans une chambre.'*

factors, but the fact that my daughter was at the Bataclan that night, and along the trajectory of those bullets, results from a conjunction of chance events. Believing that things are driven by chance is easier for me to accept than believing in some form of destiny. The idea that everything is written in advance, or governed by a form of metaphysical logic – but of what kind? – would in all likelihood make me feel more anxious rather than reassure me, which is the opposite of what a lot of people think, I suppose. It's the same when it comes to believing in an afterlife: life, real life, is here. If it's better somewhere else, then what are we doing here? I just can't see the logic in the idea of a material world created by God merely to test us.

AA: When you look up at the heavens, don't you ever dream, imagining what higher forces might inhabit them?

GS: Of course, just like everybody else! But the sense of wonder that I feel before the existence of the universe, the mysteries of life and of physics are enough to quench my thirst for spirituality. I don't need to resort to imaginary beings; just contemplating a starry sky is enough to create powerful emotions within me. When I look up at the sky, I'm not always looking for Lola's face in the stars.

AA: All the time, I feel a gnawing sense of guilt. What could I have done? It's a constant torment. Yet at the same time, as a Muslim, I believe in destiny, '*maktoub*', 'it is written' in Arabic: what has happened had to happen, sadly.

GS: But how can anybody believe in a God, and more to the point *love* a God, who would arrange the world in this way? When, in the eighteenth century, an earthquake levelled Lisbon, killing 60,000 people, the enlightenment philosophers Voltaire, Leibniz and Rousseau were already arguing about the role of God. I can see why people might say '*inshallah*' when dealing with imponderable questions, areas of reality that are foreign to us, but to go from that to putting everything in God's hands ... If there were a God, one who not only took an interest in us down here, but was also merciful, I just don't see how He could have let such tragedies take place, whether we're talking about Lisbon on 1 November 1755 at 9.40am, or the Bataclan on 13 November 2015 at 9.40pm.

AA: The expression '*inshallah*' carries two meanings: on the one hand, hope that something will happen; on the other, doubt.

GS: If everything is written, can those who have committed crimes be held responsible for their actions? This is a question which, to my mind, is akin to the doctrine of salvation through grace rather than through deeds which is accepted by some Christians. Those who have received God's grace will be saved whatever they do; those who haven't can slog away as hard as they like at being good, but access to paradise will forever be denied to them. Do you really think that what Samy did wasn't his own fault?

AA: Of course I don't, Georges! There is the idea, in Islam, that some people can be influenced by an outside force, such as *sheitan* (the Devil). But it's true that people often tend to put things down to *maktoub* ...

GS: The question of free will isn't easy to explain for atheists, either. If we're the product of our genes and our personal history, our cultural upbringing, our education and our environment, none of which are things we have chosen, how can we be responsible for what we do? To what extent do we really decide our own actions? Christians believe that God created good and evil. The existence of evil is necessary because if it were impossible to do evil, then there would be no actual free will: the definition of freedom is the ability to choose between doing good and doing evil. But in Islam and Christianity alike, how can free will be reconciled with predestination? The question remains hugely problematic.

Mourning in spite of everything

GS: Azdyne, can you pick up where you left off about your experiences post-13 November?

AA: The following days were terrible. To echo what we've just been discussing, we really did lose all control over our destiny. For Mouna, who works in the public sector, it was very hard, but she could count on the support of a number of people who refused to pass judgement on her. But Maïssa, our youngest daughter who lives in France, was ostracised overnight. After promising that they would protect her job, 'because it's important to judge people on their own merits', her employers – the Paris municipal authority – ended up letting her go. Personally, I didn't go to a therapist, as I was suffering so much that I couldn't see how a doctor could help me. What about you, did you see one?

GS: I don't think that silence and taboo are healthy ways of going about grieving ... Then again, nor are compulsively going back over memories and creating a cult to the dead person. After 13 November, my whole family went to Sainte-Anne hospital, as a group, to see a psychiatrist specialising in bereavement. She provided us with some keys to understanding what we were going through, and this group consultation allowed some of us to go further individually. Personally, I left it there.

Emmanuelle and I obviously still think about Lola. We went to the Bataclan to pay our respects as soon as we were able to. We've kept all the photos and films she appears in, but we haven't put her picture on every wall of the house, and we don't go to the cemetery every day. It's different for us; for instance, there are plenty of family meals where we don't talk about Lola. I think that's normal. At the beginning of the grieving process, the feeling of loss is terribly painful. You mustn't forget, but you must let your memory heal. This is nature's way: the wound never closes completely, but the pain lessens. You have to reconstruct your life and your personality around it. We're not in a state of pathological, invasive grief, and in any case I don't think Lola would have wanted that for us.

AA: As for me, I just went to see our family doctor and an imam, and what they said was enough for me. My wife

GEORGES SALINES & AZDYNE AMIMOUR

Mouna, though, has trouble concentrating, when she's reading or watching a film, for example.

There were days when we had almost thirty journalists camped out in front of our door; it was driving us crazy and I was afraid of possible revenge attacks. So, we preferred to hide ourselves away and bury this secret. We were able, however, to count on some of our close friends in the neighbourhood for help. When the journalists wouldn't go away, our Jewish neighbour and friend whom I've told you about, Richard, would come and block the way to our door. I heard him yell several times at people who'd come to gawp: 'Leave them alone! Stop harassing them!' He was so warm-hearted. Sadly he's died since. In our apartment block, he was like a guardian angel for us, whereas the two Arab families on our floor didn't give us any support.

GS: It's quite obvious that you should have received some help, some psychological support. You can't get through these things alone. I'll give you the number of someone who's really good. I'm going to ask a difficult question ... Even though it's forbidden in Islam, did you ever find yourself thinking about suicide?

AA: There was a time in the past when, yes, I did feel that I was being consumed by thoughts of death. But since 13 November I haven't felt that way. Given what Samy made those innocent people suffer, what I feel today above all is a sensation of disgust and hatred. When I think that it may have been Samy who killed Lola ... We'll never know, and perhaps that's for the best in a way, the suffering would be even more awful, more unbearable. And looking you in the eye and telling you this, Georges, I'm crying.

GS: We'll never know if it was Samy who ... it's true, but, you know, it doesn't make any difference for me whether the bullet which killed Lola came from the barrel of his gun or from the guns of his accomplices. All three of them are guilty of killing her, as are the people who sent them and those who assisted them.

AA: Samy was fighting a war, but the people he killed weren't. Even if it's hard for me to admit it, and even say it, I would have preferred it if he'd met his end on the frontline in Syria rather than go on to commit 'the unspeakable', to use your expression.

But I do think that Samy was manipulated and used. Daesh really know what they're doing in that respect. Might I one day have the right to claim that Samy, in a sense, was a victim who created other victims in turn? This is why I went to pay my respects at the commemoration of the first anniversary of the attack, and also contacted the families of victims from the Bataclan. Some didn't reply, others refused to speak to me, but you, Georges, you accepted my request. Some survivors also told me that they understood what I was doing, and that warmed my heart.

I also met the former journalist, now a clinical sociologist, Isabelle Seret, who was putting together a programme of web videos as part of the RAFRAP (*Rien à faire rien à perdre*, 'Nothing to do, nothing to lose') project, which seeks to raise awareness of the techniques of psychological manipulation employed by Islamic State. I offered to organise meetings between the parents of victims and the parents of jihadists, and from these emerged the group *Retissons le lien* ('Let's Rebuild Connections'), which held its first public event in Belgium in 2019. Like Saliha Ben Ali, whom we've already mentioned, I felt I absolutely had to do something, not sink into despair, but rather contribute in whatever way I could.

GS: In my previous book, I wrote that I saw the perpetrators as being victims too, even if people generally still have trouble accepting this. This is a complex issue: while it's important not to ignore the role of psychological manipulation in jihadism, it's also crucial to accept the idea that each of us bears responsibility for our acts.

Without proof to the contrary, the families of jihadists cannot be considered to be guilty, and their suffering must be recognised. Reason tells us this, but there's reason and there's ... emotion: it's hard for victims' loved ones to understand the suffering experienced by the families of terrorists. In all honesty, though, I'm not sure that the suffering of the former is, by its very nature, necessarily greater than that of the latter. I'm sometimes called an Islamo-leftist for saying this sort of thing, but parents cannot be held responsible for the actions of their children. In certain families, there can be a degree of cultural approval, at least on an intellectual level, although this is rather rare. But I can see that you and Mouna, on the contrary, were totally opposed to intolerance, sectarianism and violence, and can't be blamed for your son's misdeeds.

There are many parents out there who need to see that your story is directly relevant to them, and they should not think that they would never be faced with such a situation. Samy criticised you for not being good Muslims, but if you had been more devout, you would no doubt have been accused of providing fertile ground for your son's descent into evil. It's true that in the values you handed down to your family, Azdyne, there may have been a certain propensity to take conspiracy theories seriously, and some communication problems within the family; it's true that your frequent absences may have had an effect on Samy's behaviour; but does someone become a terrorist just because of that? How many families are completely devoid of faults?

Determinism has its limits as a theory: young people with a similar upbringing do not all become jihadists, which is just as well. And this is the difference between responsibility and guilt. External factors were obviously involved, factors which no one had the power or the necessary knowledge to control or prevent. In his quest for something which he himself was perhaps unable to define, Samy came into contact with the wrong people at the wrong time and fell into the abyss.

AA: You are an exceptional human being, Georges. Many people, I suspect, would be more judgemental, and I can understand why.

GS: My philosophy is that of the rule of law, and of respect for justice and its institutions. The death penalty and perpetual imprisonment no longer exist, and I think that our democracies must keep moving in this direction. Revenge is an illusion.

AA: Is that why you took on a public role as a representative of the victims' families?

GS: Whereas my wife turned her attention towards activities that had absolutely no connection with the topic of terrorism, I threw myself headlong into the subject. After the events, I decided to carry on responding to requests from the media in order to call for a national effort: why did this tragedy happen to us in France? How can we effectively combat the scourge of jihadist terrorism?

We got in touch with other victims' support organisations and, in December 2015, went to meet 'Paris aide aux victimes' (Paris Victims' Support). This organisation is part of 'France Victimes', the network of non-governmental support groups set up by the former justice minister, Robert Badinter, in 1980. In each of France's departments, there is a group offering legal and psychological support to the victims of crimes of any sort. Through this organisation, we submitted our application to be officially recognised as 'victims' in order to qualify for the reimbursement of funeral costs and arrange for our representation as plaintiffs at the criminal trial. Alongside this, the National Federation for Victims of Terror Attacks and Disasters (Fenvac) organised a meeting with a view to founding an organisation for the victims of 13 November 2015, which I attended. I met around fifteen other participants, some of them grieving family members like myself, but also survivors and parents of survivors.

AA: Setting up an organisation like this is a delicate job when you're dealing with traumatised people.

GS: Yes, and the grieving parents were all in a pretty bad place. Fortunately, there were some determined and competent young people among us, like Emmanuel Domenach and Aurélia Gilbert, two survivors from the Bataclan.

We started by each telling our story, getting to know each other and getting some idea of the scale of the problems we were experiencing, which were deep. A draft of the organisation's statutes had already been prepared, we finalised these and defined our many objectives: establish a framework within which people can come together to meet, exchange ideas, and help each other; listen to victims' needs and problems in order to provide them with support; stand with them in defending their rights and interests; work to bring the truth about the attacks to light, whether in a judicial or extrajudicial context, etc.

Perhaps because I had already spent a brief spell in the media spotlight in November, I was asked, as the father of a victim killed in the attack, to act as the president of the organisation, which we called '13eleven15' (*13onze15*), founded on 9 January 2016. An article about us was published in *Le Parisien* newspaper and, despite only having a makeshift office and very little experience, we rapidly became the focus of an impressive amount of media coverage and political interest. The parliamentary inquiry commission, the president's office, the justice and interior ministers, the media ... I found myself thrust in front of the cameras, addressing large meetings, or face-to-face with important figures. It wasn't easy.

AA: It was very brave of you ...

GS: ... or irresponsible, but I hardly had any time to think about this: very soon, we had hundreds of official members. Every time I spoke publicly, I hammered home the message that the terrorists were trying to sow division between French citizens, and that we must not let this strategy succeed.

We replied to all the enquiries we received from the authorities and often requested meetings with political decision-makers, particularly on the subject of victims' medical costs. The health minister at the time, Marisol Touraine, made a commitment that these would be fully covered by the government. However, the devil (or *sheitan*!) was in the details: the 100 per cent level of reimbursement only applied to treatment covered by the Social Security system, and in France psychological therapy is only covered if it is provided by a registered doctor, or in a hospital setting. Psychoanalytical treatment provided by psychologists who are not doctors, for example, is not covered, and nor are psychiatrists' charges above a set level. We managed to make some progress on all these questions. In parallel, we also worked on helping victims with housing issues and the problems they faced in returning to work.

AA: I've heard that certain people have tried to pass

themselves off as victims. Have you ever encountered this?

GS: There is a master list of victims held by the court and the state prosecutor for the Republic, but it's not an absolute guarantee against impostors. The authorities have trouble unmasking them, as they can quickly find themselves accused of being overly suspicious and harassing genuine victims with demands for documents or other proof. There have indeed been cases of false victims, including some who have joined victims' groups: some are con-artists, but there are also what I would call mythomaniacs, people passing themselves off as victims who in some cases seem to believe their own lies, and appear to be looking for an identity, a family. Voluntary organisations like ours have even less power to expose them than the authorities; we just have to trust people and we don't ask them to produce a ticket for the Eagles of Death Metal concert. False victims have managed to get into some groups; some have even had official roles within them. Barring any new nasty surprises, which with any luck are becoming more and more unlikely as time goes on, they've all been unmasked, and those who tried to derive financial gain from their activities have been prosecuted.

AA: How involved are you in commemorative activities?

GS: We participate in the special days of commemoration paying tribute to victims. The first one we took part in was held on 19 September 2016 at the Invalides, organised by the Fenvac and the AFVT (*Association française des victimes du terrorisme*, French Association for Victims of Terrorism), and attended by the president of the Republic. I gave a speech on behalf of 13eleven15 at the event. And every year since 2016, we have taken part in the ceremonies organised on 13 November. In 2016, these anniversary commemorations were marked by the inauguration of plaques in memory of the victims at the Stade de France, the restaurant terraces in the 10th and 11th *arrondissements* and the Bataclan. Currently, our memorial commission and that of another organisation, Life for Paris, are working with the Inter-Ministerial Delegation for Assistance to Victims and the Paris Town Hall with a view to erecting a monument to the victims of 13 November.

There have also been many commemorative initiatives which are more specific to the memory of individual victims. For example, at the National Centre for the Book, there is a plaque in memory of Lola and Ariane Theiller, the two editors who died that day, and we lend our support to some individual parents who have created local groups.

AA: Do you ever fear that at some point you might be used for political ends?

GS: Of course, it's a constant worry and we have it written into our statutes that we are forbidden from taking party political positions. We have always given a public reaction when political personalities have claimed to speak on behalf of victims in their declarations, especially given that many have done this when they were putting forward measures that we did not support.

However, working in an organisation like ours necessarily involves dealing with the authorities, not only at the executive level of national government, but also at the local government, legislative and judicial levels. The Paris Mayor's Office has always lent us their support, providing us with premises and a grant, and hosting our conferences and general meetings. This assistance is to be expected, perhaps, but I will always be grateful to Anne Hidalgo for her material and moral support and her personal commitment.

AA: Have you met with the victims of other terror attacks, in France and abroad?

GS: Yes, of course. Creating links between all victims of terrorism is one of the most useful and important activities carried out by these groups. In France, 13eleven15 has been in contact with the many victims of the Nice attack, including the group Promenade des Anges, who like us have become part of the Fenvac. We maintain close relations with organisations representing French victims of attacks in other countries, such as the attack on the Bardo museum in Tunis in March 2015. I've also, often through the French Association for Victims of Terrorism, of which I'm also a member, met many victims of earlier attacks, some much earlier, such as the Milk-Bar bombing during the Battle of Algiers, in 1956, one survivor of which, Danielle Micel-Chich, has become a friend, and also of much more recent attacks, like Étienne Cardilès, the partner of the policeman Xavier Jugelé, who was killed on the Champs-Élysées on 20 April 2017.

Abroad, we have been helped by similar groups such as the association representing the Norwegian victims of the attacks carried out in Oslo and on the Island of Utoya by Anders

Breivik on 22 July 2011, and the American group Voices of September 11th. We have, in turn, helped our Belgian friends to create V-Europe, which brings together victims of the attacks in Brussels on 22 March 2016. Last but not least, being a marathon runner I have a particular affection for the contacts we've made with the survivors of the bomb attack which targeted spectators and runners at the finish line of the Boston marathon on 15 April 2013. Some of these survivors have become very dear friends, and I ran the 2019 Boston marathon alongside them.

AA: Have you met organisations for the families of jihadists?

GS: In April 2016, I was contacted by the British Quilliam Foundation, an organisation founded by reformed jihadists, who invited me to speak at a conference. There I met some parents of jihadists, mothers for the most part, and in particular Saliha Ben Ali, the founder of SAVE Belgium, whom we've already mentioned. It was thanks to them, and to Saliha, that I personally began my journey towards the families of jihadists.

AA: And in February 2017 I contacted you ...

GS: Yes, our first meeting left a great impression on me. I was struck by your openness and your sincerity.

Giving testimony

AA: You also spoke to me about your book that day. What drove you to write it?

GS: I needed to do it. I began writing as early as December 2015: amidst all the agitation, I needed that bubble of calm to reconnect with myself. This time when I could think about what had happened, in an almost serene state, was a daily refuge from my pain. While I was writing, I didn't cry. This is how I came to publish *The Unspeakable: An A to Z*, even if I hadn't originally intended to. I had started out writing for myself, as a form of therapy following Lola's death. I don't regret having the book published, as it acted as a doorway to a new type of activity. At the beginning of 2017, the club for the prevention of radicalisation run by the municipal authorities in Creil, a troubled town if ever there was one, came with a group of teenagers to meet me.[32] Another association invited me to come to Brest (in Brittany) and give talks in several schools where teachers wanted me to talk to their students, and in some cases where the invitation had come from the students themselves. More recently, I've visited schools at the request of the French Association for Victims of Terrorism. This type of activity is increasingly supported by the CIPDR (*Comité interministériel pour la prévention de la délinquance et de la radicalisation*, Inter-Ministerial Committee for the Prevention of Crime and Radicalisation).

AA: What do you say to the young people you meet?

GS: Above all, it's about giving my own testimony: I speak

---

32 Translator's note: see pp. 164–7 for an explanation of the ongoing 'head-scarf' controversy which first erupted in Creil in the late 1980s.

to them about Lola, show them her photos, her drawings, and point out that she is just one victim among thousands throughout the world ... At the end, I tell them about my struggle against jihadism, a struggle that can only be just, not to mention effective, if it chooses the right targets and the right methods, and I make it clear that by calling for revenge and targeting entire communities, we would be doing exactly what the terrorists want us to do. I don't hide from them the fact that this approach sometimes elicits reactions ranging from incomprehension to outright hatred. The students are well behaved, attentive and interested in our lives, in the tragedies we have been through. I also listen to what they have to say to me; we talk, we debate, and I learn something thanks to them!

AA: On the basis of this experience, do you think that prevention activities like this, but involving the families of jihadists, might be possible?

GS: There is already some reluctance to invite victims to give their testimony because of the powerful emotional charge it carries, so you can imagine how the idea of asking the parents of jihadists to give theirs might go down ... But I do think that, yes, we should involve them in prevention activities. It's still a complicated question, as each family is different: how should we deal, for instance, with families who sent money to their children in Syria? Organising meetings between victims' families and the families of jihadists would be a good thing for all concerned, even if, so far, I haven't had the courage and energy to put anything in motion. In any case, the work that you're doing in Belgium with the Let's Rebuild Connections group is very much along these lines, and is of great benefit to victims. Creating something positive through something negative is crucial, and we should import this approach into France.

AA: I'd be happy to help you do this in France.

GS: To my mind, these prevention projects are absolutely essential. I'd actually like to extend them to a wider range of people, including criminals charged with terror offences, whether in prison, awaiting judgement or already released. I'm so convinced of the importance of this area of activity that I've given up my position as president of 13eleven15 in order to devote more time and energy to it. I'm glad to see that more and more victims are getting involved in the same way; there need to be a lot more of us if we are going to have a real effect.

But the real target of my fight is the hatred directed against Muslims. Anxiety regarding their place within French society has reached alarming levels, and terrorism has been used as an argument or a justification for various forms of ostracism. I continue to think that we should, on the contrary, integrate them more closely into society. Fortunately, I'm not the only one to think this way. I've actually been surprised by how rare it is for victims to express any hatred, especially those involved in work with victims' groups. Most of those I know have remained full of tolerance and humanity.

AA: I can quite understand how some French people

might be influenced by Islamophobic discourse, as the political context over the past twenty years in France has encouraged this.

GS: I would add a little nuance to this, if only in the choice of words used. I don't use the term 'Islamophobia', which is today rejected by various people, in particular ex-Muslims such as the former *Charlie Hebdo* journalist Zineb el-Rhazoui, the journalist Mohamed Sifaoui and the politician Lydia Guirous. They argue that this notion was invented by Islamists to delegitimise all criticism of Islam, which one should on the contrary be able to criticise like any other religion. However, while it's one thing to criticise Islam, it seems quite clear to me that to portray Islam's holy texts – and the Koran in particular – as the source of terrorism, is absolutely wrong. Of course, you can find verses in the Koran which call for violence against Christians or Jews, but they can't be taken out of their context, as there are also verses in the Koran which preach tolerance. The important thing is not the text, but how one interprets it.

AA: Exactly, I was always taught that the Koran should not be read on its own; it's a complex text. Apart from the fact that there is no supreme authority to decide on the meaning of an ambiguous passage and its legal interpretation, you need to possess the necessary intellectual and theological armoury to grasp the meaning of the Koran. It can be read on several different levels, making it easy for those who say they know what it means to misuse it and lead the ignorant masses down the wrong path. That's the danger.

GS: For Islamists, the solution to every problem is to go back to a literal interpretation of the texts and an idealised version of religious practice, as followed at the time of the Prophet and his companions. The problem is that the seventh-century society which today's reactionary reformers dream of is a fantasy. It never actually existed in the way they imagine it, yet this 'Salafism' is currently dominant in the Muslim world. This situation is due in part to the influence of Saudi Arabia, as Wahhabism, which is the prototype of this desire to return to the ways of the glorious past, is the version of Islam adopted by Muhammad Ibn Saud and his successors. The country's economic power and its status as guardian of Islam's holy sites ensure its privileged position. But another important factor has been the Muslim Brotherhood movement. This organisation was founded in Egypt by Hassan al-Banna, and has given fundamentalism a political, proselytising and expansionist dimension in which, according to the circumstances, jihadism or even terrorism play an important part. The Muslim Brothers have spread across the world; they're in power in Gaza with Hamas, and in Turkey with Erdogan's AKP. In France, too, we know that the association *Musulmans de France* (Muslims of France, formerly known as the UOIF) is linked to the Brotherhood.

From our streets to Daesh

AA: Another key question is: why has Daesh singled out France in particular as a target? One reason is that its thugs have decided that the 1905 Law on the Separation of the Churches and State, also known as the Secularism Law, is, ipso facto, a law promoting intolerance and rejection. According to Daesh, 1905 has thus become an Islamophobic law ... And how many Muslims, even those who feel no sympathy with jihadists, have ended up believing this?

I'm not arguing for a specifically French form of Islam; what I'm in favour of is just Islam plain and simple. The problem is that for decades, Wahhabism and Malikism (the traditional form of Islam in the Maghreb) have been becoming increasingly radicalised, especially in Europe. There's the same problem in Belgium with all these imams being sent over from Saudi Arabia, which many people are, at last, trying to speak out about. Personally, I attend a Turkish, Hanafi mosque (the Hanafi school is one of the four Sunni schools), which feels more authentic to me. It's a form of Islam which corresponds to my own outlook; I feel that I'm practising a more humane form of Islam which shows greater compassion both to me ... and to others. The imam shows openness and tolerance and is far less full of certainties than the ones we get sent from Riyadh. I'm wary of mosques that preach in Arabic when many young people of immigrant descent are unable to read or even speak the language.

GS: I completely agree with you and all of this goes back to the question of the foreign sources of money which finance Islam. Many people misunderstand the spirit of the 1905 Law, which actually protects the freedom of worship. The state is neutral and allows everyone to practise their religion as they wish. Neutrality applies to the state, not its citizens.

This general principle was shaken by the events that took place in Creil in 1989. The headteacher of a high school in this small town in the Oise department forty miles north of Paris had excluded three girls who refused to take off their Muslim headscarf in class. Faced with the ensuing furore, the government of Prime Minister Lionel Jospin sought the advice of the *Conseil d'État*, the Republic's Supreme Court. It ruled that, as long as it did not constitute an 'act of pressure, provocation, proselytism or propaganda', and as long as it did not disrupt normal activities, the expression of religious convictions could not be forbidden in schools. An official circular was duly sent to all teachers: it was up to them to decide whether or not they accepted the *hijab* in the classroom. The state thus offloaded the decision onto teachers, placing them in an awkward position. The Islamists subsequently used the pretext of the *hijab* issue as an ideological Trojan Horse and a tool of provocation and propaganda. In 2003, the then President Jacques Chirac set up a committee headed by the chief ombudsman of the Republic, Bernard Stasi. Made up of twenty members, it was tasked with updating the Republic's thinking with respect to the principle of *laïcité*, or secularism. It did a fantastic job, but in the end the government and Parliament chose to go with a blanket ban on students wearing any 'ostentatious' religious symbols, which include the *hijab* or Islamic veil, but also the kippah and large crosses. The 2004 law allows discreet symbols of one's faith to be worn, such as small crosses, religious medallions, stars of David, or Hands of Fatima. As far as the latter are concerned, they don't really have any religious meaning: it is traditional in North Africa for women to wear a *Hamsa* or Hand of Fatima in order to 'ward off the evil eye', a practice which existed long before Islam and is today popular in Israel, both among Muslims and Jews (who call it the 'Hand of Miriam').

The law of 11 October 2010 subsequently made it illegal to cover one's face in public places. This law was brought in on the basis of security considerations, but it was obvious to everybody that it aimed to ban the wearing of the *burqa* or the *niqab*. Whichever way one looks at it, this anti-*hijab* obsession has been taken as a rejection of Islam by the French, a symbol of the Republic's intolerance, and has helped the cause of Islamist proselytism. I don't think that there have ever been as many *hijabs* worn in the street as today, and this is largely a reaction to what the Islamists have been able to exploitatively portray as interference by the state in individuals' private religious affairs.

AA: Absolutely, in general, the more they've tried to ban the *hijab*, the more it's been worn. And I think that it's just revolting how extremists have been manipulating six-year-old children into wearing the *jilbab*, here in France.

GS: It really is manipulation, since there is no religious injunction that children should be veiled. The issue has come to be used as a rallying flag to stake out territory in a war of influence. Remember what happened in 2008 with the Baby-Loup nursery case. A female employee of this privately run not-for-profit nursery in Chanteloup-les-Vignes in the department of Yvelines, west of Paris, was dismissed for wearing an Islamic head-covering, a garment expressly forbidden by the internal rules of the association which employed her. With adherence to the principles of secularism and neutrality now at stake, Baby-Loup was plunged into a maelstrom of controversy, following numerous threats and considerable pressure in support of their former employee. In the meantime, the nursery had moved to the nearby town of Conflans-Sainte-Honorine. The ex-employee took her case to the Human Rights Committee (HRC) of the United Nations, which made a declaration in 2018 stating that the dismissal constituted 'an act of discrimination on the grounds of religious convictions'.

The HRC has generally been highly critical of France over these issues but has itself also been brought into question regarding some of the positions it has adopted and its make-up. In 2018, for instance, it demanded compensation following complaints from two women who while wearing the *niqab* in France had been handed fines by the police under the 2010 law. The HRC asked Paris to review the law.

So, should people have the right to go around in public with their faces hidden in the name of religious freedom? I think that the concerns regarding public safety in this respect are quite justified. In all public places, people should be identifiable and not hide their faces. Nor is France the only country to have tried to restrict the wearing of full-face veils: they are also banned in Quebec, Denmark, Germany and certain regions of Belgium, and even in Morocco since 2017. Nevertheless, the French laws of 2004 and 2010 have been interpreted by many Muslims as Islamophobic laws . . . a godsend for Daesh, who have used them as a means of attacking France.

AA: The *burqa* makes me think of the worst images of Wahhabi Arabia or Afghan Islam.

GS: But I think that we have to avoid falling into the trap of creating provocation for its own sake, as we're starting to see the eruption of increasingly ridiculous controversies, for instance surrounding the sale of the burkini and the running *hijab* in the sports shop Decathlon. Both these cases involve a mixture of commercial opportunity and provocation on the part of Islamists, who encourage Muslim women to display their religious identity regardless of what activities they are doing. But if, by the same token, Muslim women can access sports more easily thanks to '*halal*' clothing, this can mark a first step towards a degree of emancipation.

AA: Aside from the issue of the *hijab*, France seems to me to be a country which integrates immigrants successfully; there are a large number of mixed marriages. In Britain, the government has shown a great deal of tolerance towards inward-looking communities, unintentionally encouraging the growth of communalism. However, although Islamists like the model of multicultural communalism followed in the English-speaking world, this hasn't stopped them from striking the United Kingdom in retaliation for its heavy involvement in the international coalition against Daesh.[33]

GS: The fight against fundamentalism and jihadist terrorism is a battle that we must all wage together, but one which must be led first and foremost by Muslims. I really want to make my position clear on this: no Muslim should feel responsible for crimes committed in the name of a form of Islam which is not their own, but the struggle for a peaceful and tolerant interpretation of Islam must, as I see it, be fought mainly 'from the inside'. It's hard for non-believers to explain to believers what their own sacred texts actually mean.

AA: One problem which Muslims face is the absence of authority within Islam. As a result, governments can't find people in charge to speak to. We don't actually need foreign funding, either. We can set up prayer rooms using donations from worshippers, or develop cultural centres, with cafés, bookshops, Arabic lessons to help cover basic costs. Fundamentally, we Muslims need to take back control of how our religion is organised.

Our governments also share this responsibility, as they do business with authoritarian, radical, backward-looking countries like Saudi Arabia. This is an international problem of relations between states, and all the powerful arms-producing nations are involved.

---

33 Translator's note: the multicultural approach to minority communities adopted by the UK is seen as anathema by many French commentators, who condemn it as a form of 'ghettoisation' and instead favour the universalist Republican model wherein an individual's private cultural and/or religious background is subsumed within their public role as a citizen of the Republic.

GS: It's obvious that the interference by Western nations in the Arab world and Afghanistan has ended up rebounding against us. The Americans toppled Saddam Hussein in Iraq on the basis of a lie, the notorious 'weapons of mass destruction' of which no trace has ever been found. While it's true that the interventions in Libya and Syria, in which France participated, were presented as necessary to prevent the supporters of the Arab Spring from being massacred, they were also driven by geopolitical considerations and a desire to get rid of regimes that we didn't like. We've also allowed the authorities in Bahrain to crush the revolution there with the assistance of the Saudis. Such 'double standards' feed conspiracy theories which claim that the Arab Spring was actually orchestrated by the Western governments. This is pure fantasy, as the peoples of the Arab world had good reasons to rise up, and it is more the case that Western policymakers tried to gain advantage from a situation that they themselves would never have been able to create. But this can't change the fact that the West's moral authority is currently at an all-time low in the Arab world. The Abu Ghraib prison scandal, the way in which the Iraqi prisoners were humiliated, dragged around on the end of a leash by American soldiers, and the relative impunity enjoyed by those responsible, especially higher up the chain of command, have left lasting scars. We've never learned to listen to the Middle East and understand it; we've just exploited it for our own ends.

AA: In my day, the Muslim Brotherhood was the great

radical force in the Arab world, Al-Qaeda and Daesh didn't yet exist ... And, unfortunately, the end of today's Daesh won't mean the end of jihadism.

GS: I fear you're right; the issues which fuel jihadism are still there, and not just in the Middle East. The situation in our deprived *banlieues*, including in 'the 93', your own department of Seine-Saint-Denis, to give the most frequently cited example, is a real problem. The state seems unable to offer any future to the young people who live in these ghettos without any hopes or dreams of a better life, and these pockets of poverty, of discrimination, of segregation, have been skilfully exploited by radicals of all stripes for many years now.

AA: I've seen with my own eyes how things have gone downhill in Drancy. When we first arrived in 1989, you didn't see many girls with their heads covered, and if you did, they would only be wearing a simple headscarf. Then, gradually, hidden prayer rooms began springing up in the town centre, followed by the famous mosque which Samy went to. The authorities had tried to encourage ethnic diversity in the council-owned housing blocks, with French, Arab and African tenants living side by side, but we saw the French people leave and the housing estates turned into powder kegs.

Today, the young generation worry me. They're better educated, but also prouder of their religion: 'We can hold our heads high now, we don't have to hide in the shadows any more,' say the girls wearing the *hijab*. 'We're proud of who we are. Who else is there to be proud of us, otherwise?'; 'Islam isn't just something you hold in your heart, it's a visible practice with a set of visible signs.'

GS: Could you have left Drancy?

AA: I could have. We received two offers of accommodation in new blocks, but we just couldn't leave our apartment. In spite of all we've been through, my wife wasn't ready to take this step. Our home is all she has left of her son.

GS: Do you think that it will be possible to find a way out of the current situation regarding fundamentalism and jihadism?

AA: We've got to start by strengthening education for young people who lack motivation and hope. Schools are where the values of the Republic are learned; we need to improve the way in which culture is passed from teachers to young people, and vice versa. History lessons are crucial, as is teaching about different religions.

GS: Religion is taught as part of the history and philosophy syllabus, but it's true that in schools in challenging areas, many teachers encounter difficulties when dealing with certain subjects.[34] They face violent reactions, or outright rejection from some students, especially Muslims. Approaching religion from a historical, rather than a theological, point of view can be difficult in such circumstances, in the same way that dealing with the topics

34 Translator's note: all French *lycée* students study philosophy as part of their final-year *baccalauréat* syllabus.

of reproduction and the theory of evolution can in the natural sciences.

An ambitious programme of teaching citizenship is also needed: just singing the *Marseillaise* isn't enough. We need to teach students to think critically: they need to learn how to question policies and institutions, but also keep a measured perspective and not wallow in self-hatred, which has become widespread among French people. Many nations have committed atrocities; the United States and the Arab countries were also involved in the slave trade; the United Kingdom, Spain and Portugal were colonisers too. We must look at the darker side of our history, but we must also be proud of a country which gave the world the *Declaration of the Rights of Man and of the Citizen*, the country of Victor Hugo and Émile Zola, of Louis Pasteur and Claude Bernard, of the TGV train and the Ariane space rocket, a country where we enjoy so many freedoms.

AA: My granddaughter, whom I've never met, is somewhere out in Syria. I would like to bring her back to be with me here someday, in this France which has its qualities and its faults, but which would be a place where she could live in safety. Over the past few months, I've been planning to go back to Syria to find her, but it's not proving easy.

GS: We became grandparents at almost the same time. My granddaughter, whom I'm lucky enough to have near me, helped me to survive and I try to work every day to leave a better world for her. I hope with all my heart, Azdyne, that you will one day be able to bring your granddaughter back to France to be by your side. One can debate the rights and wrongs of allowing adult jihadists to return – I'm personally in favour of repatriating all French nationals, for reasons of justice, truth, respect for the law and for victims, but also for security reasons; jihadists must be judged and punished in a way appropriate to what they've done – but we shouldn't even be asking whether we ought to bring back these children. They're innocent and we should do everything in our power to bring them back; we can't abandon them! The fact that they've been mistreated doesn't mean that they themselves will mistreat others. We mustn't ignore the risks, nor should we underestimate their capacities for resilience. Leaving them in Syria is not only dangerous for them, but also for us, as in doing so we run the risk of them coming back one day with the worst of intentions.

AA: Georges, your words have strengthened my determination to pursue this project. They give me hope, life.

GS: I've found it immensely helpful to have this dialogue with you, Azdyne, to exchange thoughts and work towards a common goal. And this is our message of hope: it is possible for us to talk.

AA: When I first contacted you, I thought that my request would be met with refusal, and today I don't regret having taken that first step. We have moved forward together, and we must continue along this path, for our children's sake. And for the sake of life itself.

Letter from Azdyne Amimour to Lola Salines

Lola, Dear Lola, Dearest Lola,

I so wish I had never had to write this letter to you.

After this long conversation with your father, I've discovered that we had many things in common: music, sport, travel, Egypt ... I know the gap that losing you has left in the lives of your friends and, above all, your parents. As a father, my heart knows this.

You left too soon, your life was stolen from you by a murderous ideology. The people who carried out these atrocities did not serve Islam. Quite the opposite: they defiled it. I ask myself why, but never find an answer. Did I fail in my job as a father? I thought I was giving my son a good upbringing ... I'm so, so, sorry Lola.

My wife, Mouna, along with my daughters join me in expressing our immense sorrow, although our tears and our prayers cannot bring you back. No more than they can our son. Nothing can make up for the loss of a loved one, but life continues, with the hope that people will fully comprehend the gravity of what has happened and be able once again to live in a spirit of fraternity. We must fight to make sure that this can never happen again.

Hope sustains life, so I keep hoping. I hope for a better world, and this is what helps me to live, every day, despite this terrible weight on my conscience.

I'm sorry, Lola, forgive us, forgive them. You will forever be in our hearts. May you rest in peace.

Azdyne Amimour

Letter from Georges Salines to Samy Amimour

Samy,

'Would you have liked to meet your daughter's murderers? What would you say to them if they were here in front of you?' On several occasions, journalists have asked me these kinds of questions. I have already written in my book *The Unspeakable: An A to Z*, while explaining my opposition to the death penalty, that yes, I would have preferred it if the terrorists had been 'apprehended, tried, and sentenced to spend many years in prison with the memory of their crimes for company. I would even like to be able to meet them and talk to them, to look them in the eye, as Pope John Paul II did with Mehmet Ali Ağca, the man who had tried to assassinate him.' As for what I would have said if such a meeting could have taken place, I can sum it up in a single word: 'Why?'

You are dead, I will never meet you, and you will never be able to answer this question, but since the opportunity presents itself here, let's try to replace this impossible face-to-face encounter with an imaginary letter.

Samy,

Right from the very first word, the exercise is proving difficult: I'm not going to put 'Dear Samy', obviously. I'm not going to call you 'Sir' either, that would be ridiculous, you're the right age to be my son. You were actually the same age as my daughter, whom you killed, you or one of your accomplices. I'm not going to berate you with some insulting epithet like 'You bastard' or 'Scumbag'. I'm too polite for that, it's not my style at all, and anyway I try never to reduce a person to the sum of their misdeeds alone. So, let's just use your first name, that'll be more neutral. But it's got a sweetness to it which just sounds wrong. 'Samy' sounds so nice. It's a diminutive, a 'pet name' as we used to say in my family. Samy, like the comedian Sammy Davis Jr; Sam, like Samantha, who bewitched me on the TV as a child, like Sam the designated driver on the French road safety ads, like my running club, the 'SAM Paris 12'. A very ecumenical name to boot: derived from Samuel, which comes from the Hebrew Shmuel, meaning 'his name is God' or 'devoted to God', adopted in America from the seventeenth century onwards by Protestants ... and now popular among French Muslims today. Seine-Saint-Denis, where you lived, is the French department with the highest number of Samys. And Amimour as well, a mixture of 'ami', 'friend' and 'amour', 'love' ... The killers who inhabit our Hollywood nightmares are called 'Freddy Krueger' or 'Hannibal Lecter', not 'Samy Amimour'.

Samy,

Pretending to write to you is particularly difficult for me because I'm convinced that there's no one there to write to: I don't believe in the immortality of the soul, in the hereafter, in heaven or in hell. If I posted it, this letter would come back to me marked 'Not known at this address'. In fact, I've never written to Lola since November 13th, unlike many grieving parents, some of whom write every day to their dead child. I don't need to write to Lola. She's here, with me, all the time, in a corner of my brain, but she can't hear me. You won't be able to hear me either, but since this is an open letter, it's actually aimed at a wider audience.

So, after three false starts, let's go.

Samy,

Why? This question has preoccupied me since November 13th: why did you and your accomplices commit these appalling crimes? You stole the lives of young people your own age, people you didn't even know, you lost your own lives in doing so, you plunged the parents and friends of those you killed, and your own parents and friends, into a nightmare, you left those who survived your bullets with permanent injuries, you sullied your religion in the eyes of the world, you put all Muslims – some of whom have paid with their lives in ghastly acts of indiscriminate revenge – in danger. All that, for what purpose?

During the massacre at the Bataclan, you told your victims that it was a response to the bombing campaign carried out by France against Islamic State. How can one deliberately kill innocent civilians as a 'counter-strike' against military operations ordered by political leaders? If this was a revenge attack, it was made on the wrong target: at the Stade de France, on the restaurant terraces and at the Bataclan, there were people who voted for Hollande, people who opposed him, others who didn't care; Muslims, Christians and athe-ists; campaigners for peace, supporters of military action and people with no opinion either way ... you made no distinction. If you can call that a strategy, it's an absurd one:

the attacks did not lead to the withdrawal of French forces from Syria. Quite the opposite: they provided a justification for the military intervention and played a major role in bolstering its popularity in France. As things stand today, regardless of developments in the military situation in the Middle East, we haven't seen the end of jihadist terrorism, over which Islamic State does not hold a monopoly. But this continuing terrorism has not achieved any other feasible, 'rational' goals, either. The religious war has not happened and will not happen. Since 2015, non-Muslim French people have, on average, become more tolerant towards Muslims. The vast majority of Muslims, for their part, reject violence and terrorism. Your friends can carry on pointlessly spilling blood and spreading pain, they won't achieve their ends. Terrorism is a tactic which rarely pays off.

Of course, trying to argue this from a rational point of view probably won't work. If you could answer me, you would probably talk about the Koran, the Sunnah and your reading of these texts instead. You would tell me that you were told to fight by God Himself. Maybe you would quote the beginning of verse 5 of the ninth surah: 'But when the forbidden months are past, then fight and slay the Pagans wherever ye find them, and seize them, beleaguer them, and lie in wait for them in every stratagem (of war)',[35] ignoring the context of this surah which was 'revealed' while the Prophet was leading his troops to war. You would probably

---

35 *The Holy Qur'an*, translated by Abdullah Yusuf Ali (1934).

neglect to mention the end of the verse: 'but if they repent, and establish regular prayers and practise regular charity, then open the way for them: for Allah is Oft-forgiving, Most Merciful.' Why didn't you give your victims the chance to repent? And why has your version of Islam latched onto this verse, and others of a similar tenor, which always happen to be difficult to translate and interpret? In doing so it ignores all those who preach tolerance and, above all, call upon men, and even the Prophet himself, not to take the place of God by judging and meting out punishment in His stead. 'The Messenger's duty is but to proclaim (the message)' (5:99); 'If it had been Allah's plan, they would not have taken false gods: but We made thee not one to watch over their doings, nor art thou set over them to dispose of their affairs' (6:107); 'If one amongst the Pagans ask thee for asylum, grant it to him, so that he may hear the word of Allah, and then escort him to where he can be secure. That is because they are men without knowledge' (9:6); 'If it had been thy Lord's will, they would all have believed, – all who are on earth! wilt thou then compel mankind, against their will, to believe!' (10:99).

I'm not a Muslim, I'm not an Islamologist, I don't even believe in God. I'm not going to tell you which version of Islam is the right one from a theological point of view. But what I do know, as a human being, is that there are believers belonging to all religions, including Islam, who understand God's message as a command to do good, to love one's neighbour, to behave with decency. Who also recognise that one can doubt, make mistakes, hesitate ... And one also finds, in all religions, those who simply use their sacred text or the teachings of their preachers to provide justification for their intolerance and their violence.

Samy, why did you make the wrong choice?

Your father says that while he had every reason to turn bad, this was not the case for you. By that he means that he has had a tough life, particularly during his childhood and when he was young, and that he has faced injustice and discrimination, in particular from the French colonial authorities. You, on the other hand, were a cosseted child, surrounded by the affection of your family and raised in a favourable environment, both in material and cultural terms. I fear that these two observations, however true they may be, won't help us much in explaining what happened: radicalisation does not automatically stem from material hardship or even from injustice. And Azdyne, dear man that he is, was never in danger of becoming a terrorist: he loves life too much, and there's not an intolerant bone in his body.

But might it be possible in spite of all that your drift towards terrorism had something to do with this father who is so endearing, so charming, whose whole life, much more than mine, is a tale of adventure? His personality has some unusual features: in his system of values, following the rules is of little importance. When it comes to achieving his goals, he doesn't baulk at taking the odd short cut. He's told me how, in the course of his adventures, he ended up forging an exam certificate to try to get into medical school and living off women. Although he's a cultured man, he's entirely self-taught, which is pretty remarkable, and although he's not a man obsessed with money, which is to his credit, he does attach some importance to the material signs of success. If at one time he felt an affinity for communism, it was more out of admiration for the individual 'success' of Georges Marchais, a manual worker turned high-profile politician, than for ideological reasons.

You were a good child. You would agree to anything (so much so that your Algerian cousins gave you the nickname 'Oui'). You were probably very fond of your father. You most likely admired him and were reluctant to oppose him head-on. But when you reached adolescence, that age when one often feels a burning need for absolute truth, when one sees everything in black and white, without nuance, and when one is unable to accept that the world isn't perfect, I suspect that you had great difficulty in unquestioningly accepting his approach to morality as your own. Maybe you took a lesson from it which he certainly hadn't wanted you to learn: it's not wrong to do things that aren't allowed if this is in order to fight against 'the system', society, oppressors, bad people, *kafirs*.

So, you chose to rebel in an area where your parents were not in a position of strength: religion. Azdyne and Mouna are Muslims through their family heritage, and are moderate both in their religious practice and their faith. It's not their main concern in life. You, however, became a 'super-Muslim', to use the term coined by the psychoanalyst Fethi Benslama. By adopting an extreme version of your religion, you put yourself in a position of superiority with respect to everyone else: teachers, police, morality, parents. Your parents most of all, perhaps, as they hadn't thought enough about religion to stand up to you effectively in this area.

This is one interpretation of the path that you took, others are possible. What influence did Kahina, the woman you married, the mother of this child who will grow up without ever knowing you, have over you? Did you feel that you were rejected in France because of your origins? What did you experience during your holidays in Algeria, which your father describes as idyllic? Did your family's willingness to believe conspiracy theories affect your judgement? Were you disappointed not to have managed to gain a university degree, and a job which you enjoyed and which would satisfy your parents' ambitions?

I don't know for sure and probably never will. I've read books by psychologists, sociologists, political scientists and Islamologists. I've attended conferences. I've listened and asked questions. I've learned all sorts of things about the different factors which can contribute to a young person's transformation into a terrorist. But as far as your case is concerned, Samy, as a particular individual rather than a generic jihadist, I still don't know what happened. Given that you can neither read what I write nor reply to it, I will probably never know. In the wonderful film by André Téchiné, *L'Adieu à la nuit*, one of the characters, Lila, is preparing to go off and take part in *jihad* with her boyfriend Alex. In the meantime, she carries on working in a care home for the elderly, where she takes care of her patients with all the love and respect that her belief system supposedly forbids her from showing to unbelievers. You were a kind boy, too, a boy who everyone liked, a boy who especially loved his cat. And then you committed the same atrocities that Lila aspires to commit in the film. Human beings truly are a mystery.

It's customary to end a letter by expressing one's best wishes to one's correspondent. But what can you wish for a dead man, especially if you're not necessarily that inclined to wish him well? I imagine that you thought you would be going to paradise, as promised in the third surah: 'Think not of those who are slain in Allah's way as dead. Nay, they live, finding their sustenance in the presence of their Lord' (3:169); 'Let those fight in the cause of Allah who sell the life of this world for the hereafter. To him who fighteth in the cause of Allah, – whether he is slain or gets victory – Soon shall We give him a reward of great (value)' (4:74). I doubt very much that you received it. Of course, I don't believe in a life to come, so I don't think that you are anywhere now. Let's suppose for a minute, though, that I'm wrong, and that the revelation is the truth. It seems to me that what you thought was 'the cause of Allah' was actually a diabolical scheme condemned by the Koran, which is not especially tolerant when it comes to the murder of innocents, as verse 32 of the fifth surah reminds us: 'If any one slew a person – unless it be for murder or for spreading mischief in the land – it would be as if he slew the whole people.' So, if 'mainstream' Islam is right, then hell awaits you, and I don't wish that upon you. In fact I don't want that to happen to anybody, quite apart from the fact that, as an unbeliever, I maybe ought to feel worried myself . . .

Samy, for my sake and for yours, I hope I'm right: we are stardust, we've had the amazing good fortune to have been alive on this blue planet. Our life down here was the one that mattered because it's the only one there is. I feel sorry that you didn't know this, sorry for you, and sorry that you did so much harm chasing after an illusion. Now you're beyond the reach of my wishes. So it's your parents, your sisters, your friends that my wishes are with. May they find reconciliation with your memory and go on their way in peace.

Georges Salines